# BRITISH WARSHIPS
# & AUXILIARIES

## 1989/90 Edition

Price
£4.50

# THE ROYAL NAVY

The coming year should mark the start of the biggest reappraisal of Western diplomacy and strategic thinking for 35 years. Whether it will is another matter entirely.

For the Royal Navy with its "new" Forward Strategy, of which more later, it may well be a traumatic experience. There is going to have to be a search for a new strategy at sea that recognises the realities of the change that is coming.

The start of that change will be made manifest some time during 1989 when the 64,000 ton carrier *Tbilisi* leaves the Soviet Black Sea Shipyard at Nikolayev for the first time.

Already storm cones are being hoisted. "The threat facing the Fleet in the late 1990s is expected to increase steadily", according to Rear Admiral Michael Layard, the Flag Officer Naval Air Command, and Cdre Robert Woodard, the Commodore Clyde, writing last year in their previous appointments as Captains in the Directorates of Naval Warfare and Operational Requirements (Sea) in the Ministry of Defence. In particular their concern centres on "the advent of the Soviet aircraft carrier with its high performance fighters . . ."[1]

The *Tbilisi's* departure on trials signals the beginning of the end of what maybe termed the "Pax Americana"—the world-wide policing role the United States has been playing since 1945.

In Britain's imperial past the "Pax Britannica" rested primarily on the slow and often poorly armed gunboats and sloops of the Royal Navy which were to be found cruising for months on end in such diverse places as the Pacific coast of South America to the rivers of East Africa to maintain the stable conditions under which trade could prosper.

Despite their obvious inadequacies as fighting ships the gunboats' activities were rarely if ever seriously opposed by other major powers—for behind them lay the might of the British battlefleet—the ultimate deterrent of its day.

For almost 20 years after the end of the Second World War America's most visible and formidable deterrent rested with the nuclear weapon-carrying aircraft of its carriers. Unlike the static Inter-continental Ballistic Missiles in their silos in the Mid-West the carriers had mobility which added enormously to the deterrent potential.

It was only the onset of the nuclear powered submarine, starting with the USS *Nautilus* in 1954, which was soon to be developed to carry long range nuclear ballistic missiles, that toppled the carrier from its place in the forefront of the West's deterrent against a nuclear conflict.

But the Western carriers still remained the prime deterrent to other forms of war for the Russians' acquisition of nuclear ballistic missile submarines effectively ruled out any deterrent role their Western counterparts, the Polaris submarines, might have had against conventional aggression.

Since 1945 hardly a year has gone by without some situation arising around the world which has called for the movement of Western carriers, if not their active participation, as in Korea, at Suez, Indonesian "Confrontation", Aden, Vietnam, the Falklands and Grenada. Since 1978 "Western carriers" should read

"American" for with the paying off that year of the previous *Ark Royal* the Royal Navy has been out of the running in the deployment of large, long range air groups at sea able to meet shore-based air forces on both equal terms and probably comparable numbers.

The possession of carriers outside the context of global nuclear war gives a nation the ability to wield influence without the involvement that comes from putting troops ashore in a foreign state. Indeed carriers in this context may arguably be seen as the embodiment of sea power and "he that commands the sea is at great liberty, and may take as much and as little of the war as he will. Whereas these, that be strongest by land, are many times nevertheless in great straits", wrote Sir Frances Bacon.[2]

Moscow should be all too well aware of this with the financial bottomless bucket of its involvements in Angola and Ethiopia where its use of Cubans as cannon-fodder has, after years of bitter fighting, still gained the Russians neither the political nor the economic influence they have sought for so long in Africa.

Certainly in many situations the Soviet Navy has been able to exert some influence, mainly on the West, merely by positioning its ships in crucial areas. But the presence for many years of a Russian naval vessel in the Straits of Hormuz at the entrance to the Gulf in no way appears to have inhibited attacks in the Gulf war on Russian flag ships. Nor did the presence of a small permanent Russian squadron off West Africa inhibit Ghana's seizure of poaching Russian trawlers.

Similarly, there was no way, even had it wished to do so (which may be questionable), that Moscow could have thwarted the American carrier air strikes on targets in Libya in 1986, short, of course, of direct hostile actions against US warships.

In the American action in removing a self-appointed Communist regime in Grenada there was nothing the Russian Navy could have done that would seriously have upset American plans.

Yet the whole raison d'etre for the postwar build up of the Soviet Navy is often attributed to the Kremlin's frustration when it was unable to inhibit American intervention in the Lebanon in 1958 and then, four years later, when it had to withdraw its missiles from Cuba under the pressure of an American naval blockade.

In each of these issues carrier air power was a decisive factor. No Soviet missile cruiser or destroyer could pack sufficient a punch to be construed by Western commanders and seen by political leaders and public as a significant counter to a US carrier task group.

The anti-ship missile armed submarine could offer a significant threat to a carrier task group. But it suffers from a grave disadvantage in situations outside a hot war: to be effective it must remain invisible and therefore at once loses any impact it might have on the media and public opinion in any confrontation. It is, moreover, in no position to operate in close proximity to a Western task group as a means of restricting its freedom of manoeuvre. Similarly, a submarine's use in a showing the flag role is likely to be quite counterproductive since its sinister appearance and inability to host numbers of visitors mean that it is more likely to be the target for "peace", "environmental" and other protesters.

The Soviet Navy's progression from the half-deck missile armed helicopters cruisers *Leningrad* and *Moskva* of 20 years ago to the first of the *Kiev* class ships with their vertical take-off Yak-36 Forger fighters in 1975 to the *Tbilisi,* which was probably ordered in 1979, shows that the approach to naval aviation at sea has been cautious and seemingly logical. But the *Tbilisi* along with her sister ship laid down in 1985 will eventually represent a major advance with an air group able, for the first time, to match the more sophisticated aircraft that might be encountered

4

in some Third World states. In short, by the time the ship is fully worked up and new aircraft are operating from her in the mid-1990s the Russians are going to have a capability they have never had before to project power around the globe in a way very comparable to that which Washington has long had with its carriers.

This must inevitably mean that in future crises Western planners will have to face up to a new and disturbing factor: Moscow's ability to deploy air power wherever it wishes. This in turn will greatly enhance its ability to intervene in support of its allies overseas and to further its own interests generally and at the same time to raise the stakes very considerably for the West, perhaps to a point where it might have to make a humiliating climb down, just as Moscow had to do in 1962.

Just as significant, particularly for Britain, is the impact the *Tbilisi* will make on current "hot war" strategy at sea, the so-called Forward Strategy. (This is really a part of the US Maritime Strategy, first made public in January 1986, under which US submarines, surface ships and aircraft in war would seek to close in on Soviet Northern Fleet bases in the Kola peninsula and those of their Pacific Fleet in the Kamchatka peninsula sweeping away any opposition before them).[3]

". . . just as on land NATO believes in forward defence; we have a strategy of forward defence at sea also. What we intend to do, and what we seek to do, is to deploy our forces in a way in which we would contain the Soviet threat as far north as possible and thereby avoid or limit the amount of that threat which comes into the vast expanse of the Atlantic itself. Basically our strategy aims to prevent the situation arising in which there is a large threat in the Atlantic sea lanes by containing Soviet maritime forces . . . in northern waters." Thus the first public mention of the Forward Strategy was spelt out to the House of Commons Defence Committee in February 1988 by the Defence Ministry's principal witness, Mr Richard Mottram, an Assistant Under Secretary.

"This is the first point", he said, and then went on to expand on the RN's role within that strategy. ". . . the Royal Navy would have a particularly important part to play at the outset since they could deploy forward into the Norwegian Sea early in a time of tension and hold the ring until the arrival of major US forces".

The nearest Russian air bases are some 400 miles from the Norwegian Sea, about the same distance over which the Argentines had to fly to attack the British task force in the Falklands War. But for two British carriers operating some two dozen Sea Harriers successfully to have won air superiority over the Argentine air force was one thing—it would be quite another matter fighting off vastly larger and better armed Soviet air forces.

Thus it would be essential that Norwegian air bases remained in Allied hands and so it would be vital for Royal Marines Commandos and their Dutch compatriots in the UK Netherlands Landing Force to be got ashore as quickly as possible by the RN's amphibious ships to help defend these airfields.

Later in the same hearing in which Mr Mottram outlined the new Forward Strategy the Defence Committee MPs were also told that the threat Soviet aircraft would pose to shipping in the Atlantic in war would be "very minimal", according to a senior RN Captain in the MoD. The Soviet planes would have first to cross the UK air defence region or other areas under Allied control and thus would suffer heavy losses before reaching the Atlantic.[4]

The whole strategy locks together very neatly for the planners. The Russians sit tight in their northern bases waiting until the whole Western military machine starts rolling. Commandos come ashore in Norway and ships start shuttling across the Atlantic carrying supplies and reinforcements for Allied forces in Europe.

At last the Russians wake up and immediately start trying to attack these Allied

ships in the Atlantic. But to their dismay their own forces are penned in by a ring of steel. Their submarines are trapped by the RN ships and submarines deployed close to their ports and their aircraft are unable to get past the massed squadrons of defending aircraft which have turned the UK into one huge unsinkable aircraft carrier.

If such a scenario bore the slightest relation to reality it must be questioned why the Russians have bothered at such enormous cost to build themselves an ocean-going fleet over the past 40 years.

Rather, they have realised that a fleet on the one hand gives them the ability to defend "mother Russia" far beyond her coasts and on the other that they now have a means of projecting power and influence around the globe. Ingrained in the mind of every Russian is the knowledge that in the Second World War 20 million Russians died. Avoidance of this level of loss—by keeping a conflict as far away as possible from the homeland—must therefore be a paramount factor in Russian military thinking.

Such thinking is most unlikely to want to see the world's largest navy confined and skulking in its bases and exercising at most only a coast defence role in war.

The new ability to deploy air power far beyond the reach of its land-based planes that the Kremlin will soon have with its carriers and long range bombers like the supersonic "Backfire" mean that there will no longer be sea areas where Western planners can confidently claim the air threat is "minimal".

Obviously with initially only two carriers this new found capability for the Soviet Navy will be limited. But then at no time during World War II did the Germans have more than three battleships operational and for much of the war they had only one—yet these tied down four times the number of British capital ships.

No doubt it will in due course be claimed that the US Navy will keep constant tabs on the Soviet carriers and, just as once Mr Healey, the then Labour Defence Secretary, claimed Allied shore based aircraft would sink every Russian warship in the Mediterranean in six hours, so, too, the Russian ships would survive only a matter of hours in war.

But such an argument is a two-edged one. If satellite reconnaissance makes it possible to track major naval units at all times, itself a still dubious claim, then the Soviet Ocean Surveillance System integrating a variety of intelligence gathering sources is almost certainly superior and more comprehensive than anything in the West.

The *Tbilisi* and her sister ship, (the Americans indicate that they expect others to be built), will carry 65-70 aircraft. Initially these will probably be subsonic, limited range Yak-36 vertical take-off fighters of inferior performance to the Sea Harrier, and at sea in the earlier *Kiev* class ships. An improved version, the Yak-41, is under development for carrier flying.

But more importantly the Su-27, a conventional interceptor with a speed of Mach 2, has been seen undergoing tests ashore using a "ski jump" ramp like that fitted in the RN's *Invincible* class carriers. The *Tbilisi* has a "ski jump" and arrester wires for handling conventional aircraft. Later she may possibly be fitted with aircraft launching catapults and these may be installed from the start in the second and any subsequent ships of the class. The *Tbilisi* was built in a drydock in which her sister ship is now building and with only one such dock in the Soviet Union production rate of these carriers would be only one every four or five years.

As in the 28,000 ton battlecruiser *Kirov*, completed in 1980 (and since joined by a sister ship the *Frunze* and with two more sister ships building) the *Tbilisi* will be

---

**Opposite: The other side of the coin . . . The Soviet carrier KIEV.**

7

powered by a combination of nuclear reactors and oil-fired boilers to generate steam for her turbines. This will give her a far greater range than the earlier *Kiev* class ships and it seems likely she and other carriers of the class will form task groups with *Kirov* class ships. This will go some way to offset the Soviet Navy's lack of tankers designed for replenishing warships at sea. It should be noted that only five of the US Navy's 15 carriers are nuclear powered, although two more nuclear powered carriers are due for completion at the end of 1989 and in 1991.

In terms of resources to match this newly developing threat Captains Layard and Woodard see the need for "a further increase in the capability of the Sea Harrier if a shortfall is not to exist". Under the present modernisation plans the Sea Harrier is to get new American (AMRAAM) air-to-air missiles and a new radar and these and other improvements in the weapon system would be the basis for the next generation of naval aircraft which, unlike the Sea Harrier, would have to be supersonic and with a greater range. "We firmly believe that vertical landing is the key to flexibility of operations, not only for shipborne users of aircraft but also for all tactical land based operations as well . . . It is a great pity that the United Kingdom has not invested already in advanced VSTOL (Vertical/Short Take-off and Landing) designs; we have an acknowledged world lead in this with the Harrier and Sea Harrier, one of the world's most versatile and battle proven aircraft, not expensive by modern standards and with update programmes that are going to make them the envy of many of the world's Air Forces".

Clearly, the new Russian carriers are going to have a big impact on future development of naval aircraft in Britain.

Second, both the British Forward Strategy and the wider US "Maritime Strategy" to which it is linked will have to be recast drastically once Moscow has the ability to deploy air power where it pleases far beyond its own shores.

Finally, the displays of force or even just the announcement of the movements of US carrier task groups may no longer have the impact they enjoy today. The influence Washington has long been able to wield with its carriers stems very largely from the knowledge among those whom it is intended to impress that Moscow is unable to make a similar and credible response.

But in future Moscow will indeed be able to make a similar kind of response in a crisis. Whether this will increase or lessen international tension is a perception dependent mainly, perhaps, upon one's political viewpoint. But what is profoundly significant is that the Russians have made clear their intention to retain their base at Cam Ranh Bay in Vietnam, regardless of what settlement may be reached by the Vietnamese government with its neighbours. This American built base is virtually the only one readily available overseas to the Soviet Navy which could support a ship the size of the *Tbilisi* and at the same time provide the runways and logistic back-up for her aircraft.

The 1990s therefore promise more change and uncertainty for the Royal Navy and those of our Allies than at any time since the 1950s. For the ultimate survival of an island industrial nation like Britain it must profoundly be hoped both the political and the naval leadership is up to the challenge that will soon be emerging.

**NOTES**

1. "Fly Navy"—The Journal of the Fleet Air Arm Officers' Association. Summer 1988.
2. "Of the True Greatness of Kingdoms and Estates". 1597.
3. "The Maritime Strategy" by Admiral James D. Watkins, USN. US Naval Institute. January 1986.
4. "The Future Size and Role of the Royal Navy's Surface Fleet". House of Commons. Defence Committee Sixth Report. June 1988. HMSO. 309. £12.70.

# SHIPS OF THE ROYAL NAVY — PENNANT NUMBERS

| Ship | Penn. No. | Ship | Penn. No. |
|---|---|---|---|
| **Aircraft Carriers** | | SCYLLA | F71 |
| INVINCIBLE | R05 | ARIADNE | F72 |
| ILLUSTRIOUS | R06 | CHARYBDIS | F75 |
| ARK ROYAL | R07 | CUMBERLAND | F85 |
| | | CAMPBELTOWN | F86 |
| **Destroyers** | | CHATHAM | F87 |
| BRISTOL | D23 | BROADSWORD | F88 |
| BIRMINGHAM | D86 | BATTLEAXE | F89 |
| NEWCASTLE | D87 | BRILLIANT | F90 |
| GLASGOW | D88 | BRAZEN | F91 |
| EXETER | D89 | BOXER | F92 |
| SOUTHAMPTON | D90 | BEAVER | F93 |
| NOTTINGHAM | D91 | BRAVE | F94 |
| LIVERPOOL | D92 | LONDON | F95 |
| MANCHESTER | D95 | SHEFFIELD | F96 |
| GLOUCESTER | D96 | COVENTRY | F98 |
| EDINBURGH | D97 | CORNWALL | F99 |
| YORK | D98 | PENELOPE | F127 |
| CARDIFF | D108 | AMAZON | F169 |
| | | ACTIVE | F171 |
| **Frigates** | | AMBUSCADE | F172 |
| ACHILLES | F12 | ARROW | F173 |
| EURYALUS | F15 | ALACRITY | F174 |
| CLEOPATRA | F28 | AVENGER | F185 |
| ARETHUSA | F38 | NORFOLK | F230 |
| SIRIUS | F40 | MARLBOROUGH | F231 |
| PHOEBE | F42 | | |
| MINERVA | F45 | **Submarines** | |
| DANAE | F47 | ODIN | S10 |
| JUNO | F52 | OLYMPUS | S12 |
| ARGONAUT | F56 | OSIRIS | S13 |
| ANDROMEDA | F57 | ONSLAUGHT | S14 |
| HERMIONE | F58 | OTTER | S15 |
| JUPITER | F60 | ORACLE | S16 |

| Ship | Penn. No. | Ship | Penn. No. |
|---|---|---|---|
| OCELOT | S17 | LEDBURY | M30 |
| OTUS | S18 | CATTISTOCK | M31 |
| OPOSSUM | S19 | COTTESMORE | M32 |
| OPPORTUNE | S20 | BROCKLESBY | M33 |
| ONYX | S21 | MIDDLETON | M34 |
| RESOLUTION | S22 | DULVERTON | M35 |
| REPULSE | S23 | BICESTER | M36 |
| RENOWN | S26 | CHIDDINGFOLD | M37 |
| REVENGE | S27 | ATHERSTONE | M38 |
| UPHOLDER | S41 | HURWORTH | M39 |
| CHURCHILL | S46 | BERKELEY | M40 |
| CONQUEROR | S48 | QUORN | M41 |
| COURAGEOUS | S50 | BRERETON | M1113 |
| TRENCHANT | S91 | BRINTON | M1114 |
| TALENT | S92 | WILTON | M1116 |
| TRIUMPH | S93 | CUXTON | M1125 |
| VALIANT | S102 | GAVINTON | M1140 |
| WARSPITE | S103 | HUBBERSTON | M1147 |
| SCEPTRE | S104 | IVESTON | M1151 |
| SPARTAN | S105 | KEDLESTON | M1153 |
| SPLENDID | S106 | KELLINGTON | M1154 |
| TRAFALGAR | S107 | KIRKLISTON | M1157 |
| SOVEREIGN | S108 | NURTON | M1166 |
| SUPERB | S109 | SHERATON | M1181 |
| TURBULENT | S110 | UPTON | M1187 |
| TIRELESS | S117 | WALKERTON | M1188 |
| TORBAY | S118 | SOBERTON | M1200 |
| SWIFTSURE | S126 | SANDOWN | M101 |
|  |  | WAVENEY | M2003 |
| **Assault Ships** |  | CARRON | M2004 |
| FEARLESS | L10 | DOVEY | M2005 |
| INTREPID | L11 | HELFORD | M2006 |
|  |  | HUMBER | M2007 |
| **Minesweepers** |  | BLACKWATER | M2008 |
| **& Minehunters** |  | ITCHEN | M2009 |
| BRECON | M29 | HELMSDALE | M2010 |

| Ship | Penn. No. | Ship | Penn. No. |
|---|---|---|---|
| ORWELL | M2011 | TRUMPETER | P294 |
| RIBBLE | M2012 | JERSEY | P295 |
| SPEY | M2013 | GUERNSEY | P297 |
| ARUN | M2014 | SHETLAND | P298 |
| | | ORKNEY | P299 |
| **Patrol Craft** | | LINDISFARNE | P300 |
| PEACOCK | P239 | | |
| PLOVER | P240 | **Survey Ships & RN** | |
| STARLING | P241 | **Manned Auxiliaries** | |
| SENTINEL | P246 | BRITANNIA | A00 |
| CORMORANT | P256 | GLEANER | A86 |
| HART | P257 | MANLY | A92 |
| LEEDS CASTLE | P258 | MENTOR | A94 |
| REDPOLE | P259 | MILBROOK | A97 |
| KINGFISHER | P260 | MESSINA | A107 |
| CYGNET | P261 | ROEBUCK | A130 |
| PETEREL | P262 | HECLA | A133 |
| SANDPIPER | P263 | HECATE | A137 |
| ARCHER | P264 | HERALD | A138 |
| DUMBARTON | | ENDURANCE | A171 |
|   CASTLE | P265 | ETTRICK | A274 |
| BITER | P270 | ELSING | A277 |
| SMITER | P272 | IRONBRIDGE | A311 |
| PURSUER | P273 | BULLDOG | A317 |
| ANGLESEY | P277 | IXWORTH | A318 |
| ALDERNEY | P278 | BEAGLE | A319 |
| BLAZER | P279 | FAWN | A335 |
| DASHER | P280 | DATCHET | A357 |
| ATTACKER | P281 | CHALLENGER | K07 |
| CHASER | P282 | | |
| FENCER | P283 | | |
| HUNTER | P284 | | |
| STRIKER | P285 | This book is updated and re-issued every *December*. Keep up to date . . . Don't miss the new edition. | |
| PUNCHER | P291 | | |
| CHARGER | P292 | | |
| RANGER | P293 | | |

**HMS Renown**

## RESOLUTION CLASS

| Ship | Pennant Number | Completion Date | Builder |
|------|----------------|-----------------|---------|
| RESOLUTION | S22 | 1967 | Vickers |
| REPULSE | S23 | 1968 | Vickers |
| RENOWN | S26 | 1968 | C. Laird |
| REVENGE | S27 | 1969 | C. Laird |

**Displacement** 8,400 tons (submerged) **Dimensions** 130m x 10m x 9m **Speed** 25 knots **Armament** 16 Polaris Missiles, 6 Torpedo Tubes **Complement** 147 (x 2).

**Notes**
These four nuclear-powered Polaris submarines are the United Kingdom's contribution to NATO's strategic nuclear deterrent. At least one of them is constantly on patrol and because of their high speed, long endurance underwater, and advanced sonar and electronic equipment they have little fear of detection.

Each submarine carries 16 Polaris two-stage ballistic missiles, powered by solid fuel rocket motors, 9.45 metres long, 1.37 metres diameter and weighing 12,700 kilogrammes with a range of 2,500 miles. The first of a new Vanguard Class was laid down in December 1986 and the second ordered in October 1987. They will carry the Trident missile.

● HMS NEPTUNE

## VALIANT CLASS

**HMS Courageous**

| Ship | Pennant Number | Completion Date | Builder |
|------|----------------|-----------------|---------|
| CHURCHILL | S46 | 1970 | Vickers |
| CONQUEROR | S48 | 1971 | C. Laird |
| COURAGEOUS | S50 | 1971 | Vickers |
| VALIANT | S102 | 1966 | Vickers |
| WARSPITE | S103 | 1967 | Vickers |

**Displacement** 4,900 tons dived **Dimensions** 87m x 10m x 8m **Speed** 28 knots + **Armament** 6 Torpedo Tubes **Complement** 103.

## Notes
DREADNOUGHT—the forerunner of this class—is awaiting disposal (by scrap or sinking) at Rosyth. These boats are capable of high underwater speeds and can remain on patrol almost indefinitely. They are able to circumnavigate the world without surfacing. Cost £24-£30 million each to build.

SUBMARINES

13

**HMS Superb**

## SWIFTSURE CLASS

| Ship | Pennant Number | Completion Date | Builder |
|------|---------------|----------------|---------|
| SCEPTRE | S104 | 1978 | Vickers |
| SPARTAN | S105 | 1979 | Vickers |
| SPLENDID | S106 | 1980 | Vickers |
| SOVEREIGN | S108 | 1974 | Vickers |
| SUPERB | S109 | 1976 | Vickers |
| SWIFTSURE | S126 | 1973 | Vickers |

**Displacement** 4,500 tons dived **Dimensions** 83m x 10m x 8m
**Speed** 30 knots + dived **Armament** 5 Torpedo Tubes **Complement** 116.

### Notes
A follow-on class of ships from the successful Valiant Class.
These submarines have an updated Sonar and Torpedo system.
SCEPTRE is now based at Faslane and others will move north
(from Devonport) in due course.

**HMS Trafalgar**

## TRAFALGAR CLASS

| Ship | Pennant Number | Completion Date | Builder |
|------|----------------|-----------------|---------|
| TRENCHANT | S91 | 1989 | Vickers |
| TRAFALGAR | S107 | 1983 | Vickers |
| TURBULENT | S110 | 1984 | Vickers |
| TIRELESS | S117 | 1985 | Vickers |
| TORBAY | S118 | 1986 | Vickers |
| TALENT | S92 | 1990 | Vickers |
| TRIUMPH | S93 | Building | Vickers |

**Displacement** 4,500 tons **Dimensions** 85m x 10m x 8m **Speed** 30 + dived **Armament** 5 Torpedo Tubes **Complement** 125.

## Notes
Designed to be considerably quieter than previous submarines. Hull is covered with noise reducing tiles. These boats also have a greater endurance & speed than their predecessors. Cost £200 million + each.

15

● VSEL

**HMS Upholder**

## UPHOLDER CLASS

| Ship | Pennant Number | Completion Date | Builder |
|------|----------------|-----------------|---------|
| UPHOLDER | S41 | 1989 | Vickers |
| UNSEEN | S42 | Launched 14·11·89. | Cammel Laird |
| URSULA | S43 | | Cammel Laird |
| UNICORN | S44 | | Cammel Laird |

**Displacement** 2,400 tons **Dimensions** 70m x 8m x 5m **Speed** 20 knots Dived **Armament** 6 Torpedo Tubes: Sub Harpoon missile **Complement** 44.

### Notes
A new class of non-nuclear submarine. The last three named will not be in service until the 1990's. Completion of UPHOLDER delayed by 3 month industrial dispute at the builders in 1988.

**HMS Opportune**

## OBERON CLASS

| Ship | Pennant Number | Completion Date | Builder |
|------|---------------|-----------------|---------|
| ODIN | S10 | 1962 | C. Laird |
| OLYMPUS ● | S12 | 1962 | Vickers |
| OSIRIS ● | S13 | 1964 | Vickers |
| ONSLAUGHT | S14 | 1962 | Chatham D'yard |
| OTTER ● | S15 | 1962 | Scotts |
| ORACLE | S16 | 1963 | C. Laird |
| OCELOT | S17 | 1964 | Chatham D'yard |
| OTUS | S18 | 1963 | Scotts |
| OPOSSUM ● | S19 | 1964 | C. Laird |
| OPPORTUNE | S20 | 1964 | Scotts |
| ONYX | S21 | 1967 | C. Laird |

**Displacement** 2,410 tons (submerged) **Dimensions** 90m x 8m x 5m **Speed** 12 knots surface, 17 knots submerged **Armament** 8 Torpedo Tubes **Complement** 70.

**Notes**
● are fitted with new bow sonars—and others will follow. 2 Stern TT removed in some boats. OLYMPUS was due to pay off in late 1988 but will remain in service until at least mid 1989. ORPHEUS was reduced to a static training vessel in late 1987.

**HMS Invincible**

## INVINCIBLE CLASS

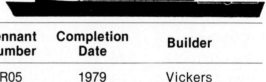

| Ship | Pennant Number | Completion Date | Builder |
|------|----------------|-----------------|---------|
| INVINCIBLE | R05 | 1979 | Vickers |
| ILLUSTRIOUS | R06 | 1982 | Swan-Hunter |
| ARK ROYAL | R07 | 1985 | Swan-Hunter |

**Displacement** 19,500 tons **Dimensions** 206m x 32m x 6.5m **Speed** 28 knots **Armament** Sea Dart Missile, 2 x 20mm guns, 2 Phalanx **Aircraft** 5 x Sea Harrier, 10 x Sea King **Complement** 900 + aircrews.

### Notes
Eventually eight Sea Harriers will be embarked in each ship—but one ship will always be in refit/reserve. INVINCIBLE completed a refit in late 1988 (3 Goalkeeper systems fitted) and will replace ILLUSTRIOUS in the operational fleet during 1989. The latter will then be placed in reserve.

**HMS Intrepid**

## FEARLESS CLASS

| Ship | Pennant Number | Completion Date | Builder |
|------|---------------|-----------------|---------|
| FEARLESS | L10 | 1965 | Harland & Wolff |
| INTREPID | L11 | 1967 | J. Brown |

**Displacement** 12,500 tons, 19,500 tons(flooded) **Dimensions** 158m x 24m x 8m **Speed** 20 knots **Armament** 2 Sea Cat Missile Systems, 2 x 40mm guns, 4 x 30mm + 2 x 20mm (INTREPID only). **Complement** 580.

### Notes

Multi-purpose ships that can operate helicopters for embarked Royal Marine Commandos. 4 landing craft are carried on an internal deck and are flooded out when ship docks down. One ship is usually in refit/reserve (currently FEARLESS). An "invitation to tender" was issued in late 1988 for an Aviation Support Ship—either a new ship or a merchant ship conversion.

19

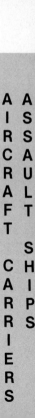

AIRCRAFT CARRIERS ASSAULT SHIPS

# DESTROYERS

**HMS Gloucester**

**HMS Bristol**

## BRISTOL CLASS (Type 82)

| Ship | Pennant Number | Completion Date | Builder |
|---|---|---|---|
| BRISTOL | D23 | 1972 | Swan Hunter |

**Displacement** 6,750 tons **Dimensions** 154m x 17m x 7m **Speed** 30 knots + **Armament** 1 x 4.5″ gun, 1 Sea Dart Missile System, 4 x 30mm + 4 x 20mm guns **Complement** 407.

### Notes
Four ships of this class were ordered but three later cancelled when requirement for large escorts for fixed wing aircraft carriers ceased to exist. Helicopter Deck provided but no aircraft normally carried. Fitted for, but not with, Vulcan Phalanx. Frequently employed as the Dartmouth Training ship for young officers.

• HMS OSPREY

## HMS Birmingham

## SHEFFIELD CLASS
## (Type 42) Batch 1 & 2

| Ship | Pennant Number | Completion Date | Builder |
|------|------|------|------|
| BIRMINGHAM | D86 ● | 1976 | C. Laird |
| NEWCASTLE | D87 | 1978 | Swan Hunter |
| GLASGOW | D88 ● | 1978 | Swan Hunter |
| EXETER | D89 ● | 1980 | Swan Hunter |
| SOUTHAMPTON | D90 ● | 1981 | Vosper T. |
| NOTTINGHAM | D91 | 1982 | Vosper T. |
| LIVERPOOL | D92 | 1982 | C. Laird |
| CARDIFF | D108 | 1979 | Vickers |

**Displacement** 3,660 tons **Dimensions** 125m x 15m x 7m **Speed** 29 knots **Armament** 1 x 4.5″ gun, 4 x 20mm guns, Sea Dart Missile System: Lynx Helicopter. 6 Torpedo Tubes **Complement** 280 +.

## Notes
Sister ships SHEFFIELD and COVENTRY lost in 1982 during the Falklands conflict. ● fitted with two Vulcan Phalanx each. A number of 30mm and 20mm guns are fitted in some ships. SOUTHAMPTON under refit/repair throughout 1989 after accident in the Gulf (Sept 1988).

**HMS Edinburgh**

## SHEFFIELD CLASS
## (Type 42) (Batch 3)

| Ship | Pennant Number | Completion Date | Builder |
|------|----------------|-----------------|---------|
| MANCHESTER | D95 | 1983 | Vickers |
| GLOUCESTER | D96 | 1984 | Vosper T. |
| EDINBURGH | D97 | 1985 | C. Laird |
| YORK | D98 | 1984 | Swan Hunter |

**Displacement** 4,775 tons **Dimensions** 132m x 15m x 7m **Speed** 30 knots + **Armament** 1 x 4.5″ gun, 4 x 30mm guns, 4 x 20mm guns Sea Dart missile system. Lynx helicopter, 6 Torpedo Tubes **Complement** 301.

## Notes
"Stretched" versions of earlier ships of the class. Extra armament (3 x 30mm weapons) fitted after Falklands crisis—but ships boats had to be removed to provide the space. Ships are designed to provide area air defence of a task force. It is planned to fit light weight Seawolf systems in due course.

23

**FRIGATES**

HMS Cornwall

● FLEET PHOTO UNIT

**HMS Brazen**

## BROADSWORD CLASS
### (Type 22) (Batch 1)

| Ship | Pennant Number | Completion Date | Builder |
|------|----------------|-----------------|---------|
| BROADSWORD | F88 | 1978 | Yarrow |
| BATTLEAXE | F89 | 1980 | Yarrow |
| BRILLIANT | F90 | 1981 | Yarrow |
| BRAZEN | F91 | 1982 | Yarrow |

**Displacement** 3,860 tons **Dimensions** 131m x 15m x 6m **Speed** 29 knots **Armament** 4 Exocet Missiles, 2 Sea Wolf Missile Systems, 4 x 30mm guns, 2 or 4 x 20mm guns, 6 Torpedo Tubes, 2 Lynx Helicopters **Complement** 224.

### Notes
Planned successor to the Leander Class. Although capable of carrying 2 helicopters, only 1 normally embarked.

25

● HMS OSPREY

**HMS Sheffield**

**BROADSWORD CLASS**
**(Type 22) (Batch 2)**

| Ship | | Pennant Number | Completion Date | Builder |
|---|---|---|---|---|
| BOXER | | F92 | 1983 | Yarrow |
| BEAVER | | F93 | 1984 | Yarrow |
| BRAVE | ● | F94 | 1985 | Yarrow |
| LONDON | ● | F95 | 1986 | Yarrow |
| SHEFFIELD | ● | F96 | 1987 | Swan Hunter |
| COVENTRY | ● | F98 | 1988 | Swan Hunter |

**Displacement** 4100 tons **Dimensions** 143m x 15m x 6m **Speed** 30 knots **Armament** 4 Exocet Missiles, 2 Sea Wolf Missile Systems, 4 x 30mm + 2 x 20mm guns, 6 Torpedo Tubes, 2 Lynx Helicopters **Complement** 273.

**Notes**
● Ships have enlarged hanger and flight deck. Can carry SeaKing helicopter if required, and eventually, the EH101.

26

W. SARTORI

**HMS Cumberland**

**BROADSWORD CLASS**
**(Type 22) (Batch 3)**

| Ship | Pennant Number | Completion Date | Builder |
|------|---------------|----------------|---------|
| CUMBERLAND | F85 | 1988 | Yarrow |
| CAMPBELTOWN | F86 | 1988 | C. Laird |
| CHATHAM | F87 | 1989 | Swan Hunter |
| CORNWALL | F99 | 1987 | Yarrow |

**Displacement** 4,200 tons **Dimensions** 147m x 15m x 7m **Speed** 30 knots **Armament** 1 x 4.5″ gun, 1 x Goalkeeper, 8 Harpoon, Seawolf, 4 x 30mm guns, 6 Torpedo Tubes, 2 Lynx or 1 Seaking helicopter **Complement** 250.

**Notes**
The gun armament & Goalkeeper added to these ships as a result of lessons learnt/re-learnt during the Falklands conflict. All these ships have major A/S capability with their latest towed array sonars. Fitted out as Flag Ships.

27

● ARTISTS IMPRESSION

**HMS Norfolk**

## DUKE CLASS (Type 23)

| Ship | Pennant Number | Completion Date | Builder |
|---|---|---|---|
| NORFOLK | F230 | 1989 | Yarrow |
| MARLBOROUGH | F231 | Building | Swan Hunter |
| ARGYLL | F232 | Building | Yarrow |
| LANCASTER | F233 | Building | Yarrow |
| IRON DUKE | F234 | | Yarrow |
| MONMOUTH | F235 | | Yarrow |
| MONTROSE | F236 | | Yarrow |

**Displacement** 3,500 tons **Dimensions** 133m x 15m x 5m **Speed** 28 knots **Armament** Harpoon & Seawolf missile systems: 1 x 4.5″ gun, 4 x 2 twin, magazine launched, Torpedo Tubes **Complement** 157.

### Notes
A new generation of cheaper (?) frigate. Costs have more than doubled from initial £67 million quoted. Major problems with ships computer assisted ops room remain to be solved.

**HMS Ariadne**

## LEANDER CLASS

| Ship | Pennant Number | Completion Date | Builder |
|------|----------------|-----------------|---------|
| ACHILLES | F12 | 1970 | Yarrow |
| JUNO | F52 | 1967 | Thornycroft |
| ARIADNE | F72 | 1972 | Yarrow |

**Displacement** 2,962 tons **Dimensions** 113m x 13m x 5m **Speed** 27 knots **Armament** 2 x 4.5″ guns, 3 x 20mm guns, 1 Sea Cat Missile system, 1 Mortar Mk10, 1 Wasp helicopter **Complement** 260.

**Notes**
JUNO (with a much reduced armament) is a training ship. DIOMEDE & APOLLO paid off in mid '88 and were transferred to Pakistan. ACHILLES for disposal during 1989.

**HMS Euryalus**

## LEANDER CLASS (Ikara Conversions)

| Ship | Pennant Number | Completion Date | Builder |
|------|---------------|-----------------|---------|
| EURYALUS | F15 | 1964 | Scotts |
| ARETHUSA | F38 | 1965 | Whites |

**Displacement** 2,860 tons **Dimensions** 113m x 12m x 5m **Speed** 29 knots **Armament** 1 Ikara Anti-submarine Missile, 2 x 40mm guns, 2 Sea Cat Missile Systems, 1 Mortar Mk10, **Complement** 240.

### Notes
6 ships were converted (1973-76) to carry the Ikara Anti-submarine Missile System (forward of the bridge) in lieu of a 4.5″ gun. The two remaining are expected to be deleted from the active fleet during 1989/90. ARETHUSA has no mortar but is fitted with Towed Array sonar. NAIAD has a static trials role at Portsmouth/Rosyth.

**HMS Charybdis**

## LEANDER CLASS
### (Sea Wolf Conversions)

| Ship | Pennant Number | Completion Date | Builder |
|---|---|---|---|
| ANDROMEDA | F57 | 1968 | HM Dockyard Portsmouth |
| HERMIONE | F58 | 1969 | Stephen |
| JUPITER | F60 | 1969 | Yarrow |
| SCYLLA | F71 | 1970 | HM Dockyard Devonport |
| CHARYBDIS | F75 | 1969 | Harland & Wolff |

**Displacement** 2,962 tons **Dimensions** 113m x 13m x 5m **Speed** 27 knots **Armament** Sea Wolf System, 4 x Exocet Missiles, 2 x 20mm guns, 6TT, 1 Lynx helicopter **Complement** 260.

### Notes
The refitting of these ships cost in the region of £70m—ten times their original cost—but they are now packed with the latest anti-submarine technology. Small calibre armaments vary between individual ships.

F47

● F.O. PLYMOUTH

**HMS Danae**

## LEANDER CLASS
## (Exocet Conversions)

| Ship | Pennant Number | Completion Date | Builder |
|---|---|---|---|
| ● CLEOPATRA | F28 | 1966 | HM Dockyard Devonport |
| ● SIRIUS | F40 | 1966 | HM Dockyard Portsmouth |
| ● PHOEBE | F42 | 1966 | Stephens |
| MINERVA | F45 | 1966 | Vickers |
| DANAE | F47 | 1967 | HM Dockyard Devonport |
| ● ARGONAUT | F56 | 1967 | Hawthorn Leslie |
| PENELOPE | F127 | 1963 | Vickers |

**Displacement** 2,860 tons **Dimensions** 113m x 12m x 5m **Speed** 27 knots **Armament** 4 Exocet Missiles, 3 Sea Cat Missile Systems, 2 x 40mm guns, 6 Torpedo Tubes, 1 Lynx helicopter **Complement** 230.

### Notes
The highly successful Leander Class are the last steam powered frigates in the Royal Navy, all later ships being propelled by gas turbines. ● ships have been refitted with Towed Array sonar and their armament reduced to 2 Sea Cat systems. The 20mm guns replaced 40mm weapons (to reduce top weight.)

**HMS Amazon**

## AMAZON CLASS (Type 21)

| Ship | Pennant Number | Completion Date | Builder |
|------|----------------|-----------------|---------|
| AMAZON | F169 | 1974 | Vosper T. |
| ACTIVE | F171 | 1977 | Vosper T. |
| AMBUSCADE | F172 | 1975 | Yarrow |
| ARROW | F173 | 1976 | Yarrow |
| ALACRITY | F174 | 1977 | Yarrow |
| AVENGER | F185 | 1978 | Yarrow |

**Displacement** 3,250 tons **Dimensions** 117m x 13m x 6m **Speed** 30 knots **Armament** 1 x 4.5″ gun, 2 x 20mm guns, 4 Exocet Missiles, 1 Sea Cat Missile System, 1 Lynx helicopter, 6 Torpedo Tubes **Complement** 170.

### Notes
These General Purpose frigates were built to a commercial design by Vosper/ Yarrow and subsequently sold to the Ministry of Defence. All of the class have been given extra hull strengthening. ARDENT and ANTELOPE lost during Falklands war.

**HMS Hurworth**

## MINE COUNTERMEASURES SHIPS (MCMV'S) BRECON CLASS

| Ship | Completion Date | Pennant Number | Builder |
|------|-----------------|----------------|---------|
| BRECON | 1980 | M29 | Vosper T. |
| LEDBURY | 1981 | M30 | Vosper T. |
| CATTISTOCK | 1982 | M31 | Vosper T. |
| COTTESMORE | 1983 | M32 | Yarrow |
| BROCKLESBY | 1983 | M33 | Vosper T. |
| MIDDLETON | 1984 | M34 | Yarrow |
| DULVERTON | 1983 | M35 | Vosper T. |
| BICESTER | 1986 | M36 | Vosper T. |
| CHIDDINGFOLD | 1984 | M37 | Vosper T. |
| ATHERSTONE | 1987 | M38 | Vosper T. |
| HURWORTH | 1985 | M39 | Vosper T. |
| BERKELEY | 1988 | M40 | Vosper T. |
| QUORN | 1989 | M41 | Vosper T. |

**Displacement** 625 tonnes **Dimensions** 60m x 10m x 2.2m **Speed** 17 knots **Armament** 1 x 40mm + 2 x 20mm guns **Complement** 45.

### Notes
The largest warships ever built of glass reinforced plastic. Designed to replace the Coniston Class—their cost (£35m) has dictated the size of the class. Very sophisticated ships—and lively seaboats! 30mm gun now in COTTESMORE—others will be retro-fitted. 20mm weapons fitted in all ships serving in the Gulf—others will follow.

● OFFICIAL PHOTO

**HMS Itchen**

## FLEET MINESWEEPERS
## RIVER CLASS

| Ship | Pennant Number | Completion Date | Builder |
|------|----------------|-----------------|---------|
| WAVENEY | M2003 | 1984 | Richards |
| CARRON | M2004 | 1984 | Richards |
| DOVEY | M2005 | 1984 | Richards |
| HELFORD | M2006 | 1984 | Richards |
| HUMBER | M2007 | 1985 | Richards |
| BLACKWATER | M2008 | 1985 | Richards |
| ITCHEN | M2009 | 1985 | Richards |
| HELMSDALE | M2010 | 1985 | Richards |
| ORWELL | M2011 | 1985 | Richards |
| RIBBLE | M2012 | 1985 | Richards |
| SPEY | M2013 | 1985 | Richards |
| ARUN | M2014 | 1986 | Richards |

**Displacement** 850 tons **Dimensions** 47m x 10m x 3m **Speed** 14 knots **Armament** 1 x 40mm, 2 x GPMG **Complement** 30.

### Notes

Built as replacements for the MCM ships serving with the RNR. BLACKWATER has an RN ships company and is in the Fishery Protection Squadron (FPS). Built to commercial specifications with steel hulls. Designed for 'sweeping in deep water. Orders for four more of this class were expected in 1987 but were not forthcoming. Older Coniston class retained in service until new vessels ordered—or task reduced.

MCM VESSELS

**HMS Sheraton**

## CONISTON CLASS

| Ship | Penn. No. | Ship | Penn. No. |
|---|---|---|---|
| BRERETON (H) | M1113 | KELLINGTON (H) | M1154 |
| BRINTON (H) | M1114 | KIRKLISTON (H) ● | M1157 |
| WILTON (H) | M1116 | NURTON (H) | M1166 |
| CUXTON (S) | M1125 | SHERATON (H) | M1181 |
| GAVINTON (H) ● | M1140 | §UPTON (S) | M1187 |
| HUBBERSTON (H) | M1147 | WALKERTON (S) ● | M1188 |
| IVESTON (H) | M1151 | §SOBERTON (S) | M1200 |
| KEDLESTON (H) | M1153 | ● In Reserve at Portsmouth | |

**Displacement** 425 tons **Dimensions** 46m x 9m x 3m **Speed** 15 knots **Armament** 1 x 40mm gun, **Complement** 29/38.

**Notes**
120 of this class were built in the early 50s but most have now been sold overseas or scrapped. They have fulfilled many roles over the years and have given excellent service. WILTON, built of glassfibre in 1973, was the world's first 'plastic' warship. Ships marked § are employed on Coastal Fishery Protection duties. Ships marked (S) are Minesweepers—(H) Minehunters. HMS ABDIEL the RN's last dedicated minelayer was sold in mid 1988.

● W. SARTORI

**HMS Sandown**

## SANDOWN CLASS

| Ship | Pennant Number | Completion Date | Builder |
|------|----------------|-----------------|---------|
| SANDOWN | M101 | 1989 | Vosper T. |
| INVERNESS | M102 | | Vosper T. |
| CROMER | M103 | | Vosper T. |
| WALNEY | M104 | | Vosper T. |
| BRIDPORT | M105 | | Vosper T. |

**Displacement** 450 tons **Dimensions** 53m x 10m x 2m **Speed** 13 knots **Armament** 1 x 30mm gun **Complement** 34.

### Notes
A new class designed to operate in deep (continental shelf) waters. Propulsion by vectored thrust and bow thrusters. Plans exist for a further 15 to be built but all the five above will not be in service until 1993.

W. SARTORI

**CASTLE CLASS**

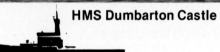

**HMS Dumbarton Castle**

| Ship | Pennant Number | Completion Date | Builder |
|------|----------------|-----------------|---------|
| LEEDS CASTLE | P258 | 1981 | Hall Russell |
| DUMBARTON CASTLE | P265 | 1982 | Hall Russell |

**Displacement** 1,450 tons **Dimensions** 81m x 11m x 3m **Speed** 20 knots **Armament** 1 x 40mm gun **Complement** 40.

**Notes**

These ships have a dual role—that of fishery protection and off-shore patrols within the limits of UK territorial waters. Unlike the Island Class these ships are able to operate helicopters—including Sea King aircraft. Trials have been conducted to assess the suitability of these ships as Minelayers. DUMBARTON CASTLE returned to UK in late 1988 after two years in the South Atlantic. Replaced in South Atlantic by LEEDS CASTLE.

**HMS Lindisfarne**

## ISLAND CLASS

| Ship | Pennant Number | Completion Date | Builder |
|------|----------------|-----------------|---------|
| ANGLESEY | P277 | 1979 | Hall Russell |
| ALDERNEY | P278 | 1979 | Hall Russell |
| JERSEY | P295 | 1976 | Hall Russell |
| GUERNSEY | P297 | 1977 | Hall Russell |
| SHETLAND | P298 | 1977 | Hall Russell |
| ORKNEY | P299 | 1977 | Hall Russell |
| LINDISFARNE | P300 | 1978 | Hall Russell |

**Displacement** 1,250 tons **Dimensions** 60m x 11m x 4m **Speed** 17 knots **Armament** 1 x 40mm gun **Complement** 39.

### Notes
Built on trawler lines these ships were introduced to protect the extensive British interests in North Sea oil installations and to patrol the 200 mile fishery limit.

39

P
A
T
R
O
L

V
E
S
S
E
L
S

**HMS Plover**

## PEACOCK CLASS

| Ship | Pennant Number | Completion Date | Builder |
| --- | --- | --- | --- |
| PEACOCK | P239 | 1983 | Hall Russell |
| PLOVER | P240 | 1983 | Hall Russell |
| STARLING | P241 | 1984 | Hall Russell |

**Displacement** 700 tons **Dimensions** 60m x 10m x 5m **Speed** 28 knots **Armament** 1 x 76mm gun **Complement** 31.

**Notes**
The first warships to carry the 76mm Oto Melara gun. They are used to provide an ocean going back-up to the Marine Department of the Hong Kong Police. The Government of Hong Kong has paid 75% of the building and maintenance costs of these vessels. Sister ships SWALLOW and SWIFT returned to UK in 1988 and were sold (Oct 88) to the Irish Navy after only 3 years RN service.

**HMS Sentinel**

## SENTINEL CLASS

| Ship | Pennant Number | Completion Date | Builder |
|---|---|---|---|
| SENTINEL | P246 | 1975 | Husumwerft |

**Displacement** 1710 tons **Dimensions** 60m x 13m x 4m **Speed** 14 knots **Armament** 2 x 40mm **Complement** 26.

### Notes
Formerly the Oil Rig support vessel Seaforth Saga. Employed in the Clyde area on Submarine escort duties—and "marking" of Soviet vessels off N. Ireland.

W. SARTORI

**HMS Blazer**

## COASTAL TRAINING CRAFT
## ARCHER CLASS

**Displacement** 43 tonnes **Dimensions** 20m x 6m x 1m **Speed** 20 knots **Armament** Nil **Complement** 14

| Ship | Pennant Number | Completion Date | Builder |
|------|----------------|-----------------|---------|
| ARCHER | P264 | 1985 | Watercraft |
| BITER | P270 | 1985 | Watercraft |
| SMITER | P272 | 1986 | Watercraft |
| PURSUER | P273 | 1988 | Vosper |
| BLAZER | P279 | 1988 | Vosper |
| DASHER | P280 | 1988 | Vosper |
| PUNCHER | P291 | 1988 | Vosper |
| CHARGER | P292 | 1988 | Vosper |
| RANGER | P293 | 1988 | Vosper |
| TRUMPETER | P294 | 1988 | Vosper |

**Notes**

In service with RNR divisions and RN University units.

42

W. SARTORI

**HMS Redpole**

## BIRD CLASS

| Ship | Pennant Number | Completion Date | Builder |
|---|---|---|---|
| CORMORANT | P256 | 1976 | James & Stone |
| HART | P257 | 1976 | James & Stone |
| REDPOLE | P259 | 1970 | Fairmile |
| KINGFISHER | P260 | 1975 | R. Dunston |
| CYGNET | P261 | 1976 | R. Dunston |
| PETEREL | P262 | 1976 | R. Dunston |
| SANDPIPER | P263 | 1977 | R. Dunston |

**Displacement** 190 tons **Dimensions** 37m x 7m x 2m **Speed** 21 knots **Armament** 1 x 40mm gun **Complement** 24.

**Notes**

PETEREL and SANDPIPER are training ships attached to the Britannia Royal Naval College at Dartmouth. REDPOLE, HART and CORMORANT commissioned into the Royal Navy in 1985 after service as RAF search and rescue craft. HART & CORMORANT are smaller craft and are based at Gibraltar. 40mm weapon removed from most ships and replaced by a boat.

43

**HMS Fencer**

## ATTACKER CLASS

| Ship | Pennant Number | Completion Date | Builder |
|------|----------------|-----------------|---------|
| ATTACKER | P281 | 1983 | Allday |
| CHASER | P282 | 1984 | Allday |
| FENCER | P283 | 1983 | Allday |
| HUNTER | P284 | 1983 | Allday |
| STRIKER | P285 | 1984 | Allday |

**Displacement** 34 tons **Dimensions** 20m x 5m x 1m **Speed** 24 knots **Complement** 11.

### Notes
Seamanship & Navigational training vessels for the Royal Naval Reserve & University RN Units. Based on a successful design used by HM Customs. Ships are based at Glasgow, Aberdeen, Southampton, London and Liverpool respectively.

● RM POOLE

**HMS Messina**

## MANLY CLASS

| Ship | Pennant Number | Completion Date | Builder |
|------|----------------|-----------------|---------|
| MANLY | A92 | 1982 | R. Dunston |
| MENTOR | A94 | 1982 | R. Dunston |
| MILBROOK | A97 | 1982 | R. Dunston |
| MESSINA | A107 | 1982 | R. Dunston |

**Displacement** 127 tons **Dimensions** 25m x 6m x 2m **Speed** 10 knots **Complement** 9/13.

**Notes**
Very similar to the RMAS/RNXS tenders. These four craft are all employed on training duties (first three named attached to HMS RALEIGH for new entry training). MESSINA is a training ship for Royal Marines based at Poole. IXWORTH (A318), ETTRICK (A274), ELSING (A277), IRONBRIDGE (A311) & DATCHET (A357) are all former RMAS tenders now flying the White Ensign.

**HMS Roebuck**

## ROEBUCK CLASS

| Ship | Pennant Number | Completion Date | Builder |
|------|----------------|-----------------|---------|
| ROEBUCK | A130 | 1986 | Brooke Marine |

**Displacement** 1500 tonnes **Dimensions** 64m x 13m x 4m **Speed** 15 knots **Complement** 47.

### Notes
Was due to replace HECLA in the Survey fleet until the latter reprieved in 1987 for further service. Fitted with the latest fixing aids and sector scanning sonar.

**HMS Hecate**

## HECLA CLASS

| Ship | Pennant Number | Completion Date | Builder |
|------|----------------|-----------------|---------|
| HECLA | A133 | 1965 | Yarrow |
| HECATE | A137 | 1965 | Yarrow |
| HERALD | A138 | 1974 | Robb Caledon |

**Displacement** 2,733 tons **Dimensions** 79m x 15m x 5m **Speed** 14 knots **Complement** 115.

### Notes
Able to operate for long periods away from shore support, these ships and the smaller ships of the Hydrographic Fleet collect the data that is required to produce the Admiralty Charts and publications which are sold to mariners worldwide. HERALD is an improved version of the earlier ships. Plans to dispose of HECLA and HECATE in 1987/8 were abandoned. HERALD replaced ABDIEL (as HQ ship) in the Gulf in early 1988 but is expected to return to UK in early 1989.

SURVEY SHIPS

**HMS Beagle**

## BULLDOG CLASS

| Ship | Pennant Number | Completion Date | Builder |
|------|----------------|-----------------|---------|
| BULLDOG | A317 | 1968 | Brooke Marine |
| BEAGLE | A319 | 1968 | Brooke Marine |
| FAWN | A335 | 1968 | Brooke Marine |

**Displacement** 1,088 tons **Dimensions** 60m x 11m x 4m **Speed** 15 knots **Complement** 39.

**Notes**
Designed to operate in coastal waters. All were to be extensively refitted to extend hull life into the 1990's but FOX paid off for Disposal in December 1988 and other refits not yet commenced. GLEANER (A86) in a small inshore survey craft based at Portsmouth.

HMS Churchill

HMS Intrepid

HMS Boxer

F92

RFA Argus

HMS Endurance

HMS Herald

HMS Hubberston

**RFA's Diligence (left) and Tidespring**

**HMS Challenger**

## SEABED OPERATIONS VESSEL

| Ship | Pennant Number | Completion Date | Builder |
|------|----------------|-----------------|---------|
| CHALLENGER | K07 | 1984 | Scott Lithgow |

**Displacement** 6,400 tons **Dimensions** 134m x 18m x 5m **Speed** 15 knots **Complement** 185.

### Notes
CHALLENGER is equipped to find, inspect and, where appropriate, recover objects from the seabed at greater depths than is currently possible. She is designed with a saturation diving system enabling up to 12 men to live in comfort for long periods in a decompression chamber amidships, taking their turns to be lowered in a diving bell to work on the seabed. Also fitted to carry out salvage work. After a series of delays in her construction and acceptance she is expected to become operational in 1989.

● HMY BRITANNIA

## HMY Britannia

## ROYAL YACHT

| Ship | Pennant Number | Completion Date | Builder |
|------|----------------|-----------------|---------|
| BRITANNIA | A00 | 1954 | J. Brown |

**Displacement** 5,280 tons **Dimensions** 126m x 17m x 5m **Speed** 21 knots **Complement** 250.

### Notes
Probably the best known ship in the Royal Navy, BRITANNIA was designed to be converted to a hospital ship in time of war but this conversion was not made during the Falklands crisis. Is available for use in NATO exercises when not on 'Royal' business. Normally to be seen in Portsmouth Harbour when not away on official duties. The only seagoing ship in the RN commanded by an Admiral.

**HMS Endurance**

## ICE PATROL SHIP

| Ship | Pennant Number | Completion Date | Builder |
| --- | --- | --- | --- |
| ENDURANCE (ex MV Anita Dan) | A171 | 1956 | Krogerwerft Rendsburg |

**Displacement** 3,600 tons **Dimensions** 93m x 14m x 5m **Speed** 14 knots **Armament** 2 x 20mm guns **Complement** 124.

### Notes

Purchased from Denmark in 1967. ENDURANCE is painted brilliant red for easy identification in the ice of Antarctica where she spends 6 months of the year. Her role is to undertake oceanographic and hydrographic surveys in the area and support scientists working ashore. A small Royal Marine detachment is embarked. Was to have been "retired early" after her 1982 season in Antarctica, but reprieved as a result of the Falklands crisis. Refitted at Devonport 1986/7. New flight deck and hangar facilities for 2 Lynx helicopters fitted.

# THE NAVY'S MISSILES

### SEA SKUA

An anti-surface ship missile. It is carried by the Lynx helicopter.

### IKARA

A rocket propelled anti-submarine missile designed to deliver homing torpedoes. It is fitted in two Leander Class frigates.

### SEACAT

A close-range anti-aircraft missile. Control is by radar tracking and visual guidance. Propulsion is by solid fuel. It is fitted in older frigates.

### SEA DART

A ship-to-air medium-range missile with anti-ship capability. Propulsion is by ramjet and solid boost. It is carried in aircraft carriers and destroyers.

### SEA WOLF

A high speed close-range anti-missile and anti-aircraft missile with fully automatic radar control and guidance. It is fitted in some frigates.

### EXOCET

A medium-range surface-to-surface missile with a very low trajectory and a radar homing head. It is carried in some frigates.

### SIDEWINDER

An infra-red homing air-to-air missile. It has a solid propellant motor and a high explosive warhead. It is carried on the Sea Harrier.

### SEA EAGLE

A long-range autonomous sea-skimming anti-ship missile. It is carried on the Sea Harrier.

### AS 12

An air-to-surface wire-guided and spin-stabilised missile developed from the SS 11. It has a range of 6,000 metres.

### SUB HARPOON

A long-range anti-ship missile launched from a submerged submarine. It is the principal anti-surface ship armament of the Fleet submarines. Harpoon is the "above water version" for later Type 22 and Type 23 frigates.

### STING-RAY

The most sophisticated homing torpedo in service. It can be fired from deck-mounted tubes or dropped by helicopter.

### POLARIS

Submarine-launched ballistic missile fitted with nuclear warheads. It has a range of 2,500 nautical miles with solid-fuel propulsion.

# THE ROYAL FLEET AUXILIARY

The Royal Fleet Auxiliary Service (RFA) is a civilian manned fleet owned and operated by the Ministry of Defence. Its main task is to supply warships of the Royal Navy at sea with fuel, food, stores and ammunition which they need to remain operational while away from base. With so few bases overseas which can be guaranteed in time of tension—let alone during any conflict it has become vital, over the years, that everything from the smallest nut and bolt to a complete aero engine is taken on any naval deployment away from our coasts. The lack of that nut and bolt could well stop a ship in its tracks—literally. Increasingly, the service also provides aviation support for the Royal Navy—together with amphibious support and secure sea transport for army units and their equipment.

The RFA is operated by the Director of Supplies & Transport (Ships and Fuel) whose directorate is one of five that comprise the Royal Naval Supply and Transport Service (RNSTS) headed by the Director General Supplies and Transport (Naval).

As the years go by, the RFA has expanded its role and the 2,500 men who man the ships of the service have proved to be adaptable as more and more is asked of them. RFA ships are manned on a very much smaller scale than the warships they support and, even with these crew limitations, they frequently impress as they undertake rôles within the fleet that would normally be asked of a frigate—complete with sophisticated equipment and much larger complement.

Despite the delays which have befallen the project 1989 will see RFA ARGUS as an operational, dare one say, warship. With ARGUS the Ministry has a very large major unit run by a small RFA crew who provide the facilities from which the Fleet Air Arm can conduct their training programmes. The Treasury must be more than pleased with the cost effective option ARGUS will doubtless prove herself to be—even though senior RN officers look at her and see a potential "drive" they will miss—in peace time at least. If war were declared ARGUS must be the first candidate to lose her blue ensign. She would doubtless be converted, more or less overnight, into a true front line aircraft/helicopter carrier. It's a strange world when a ship such as ARGUS is an RFA whereas a disarmed training frigate such as JUNO warrants warship status . . .

With RFA DILIGENCE winning high praise for her supporting role in the Gulf, and her merchant "half sister" STENA SEASPREAD in the Falklands fulfilling a vital role keeping the South Atlantic ships fully maintained so far from home large amounts of money are, quite rightly, being spent on providing "depot ships" in support of operations overseas. Many naval officers consider money should be made available for a dedicated depot ship for rapid deployment overseas when the next operational commitment comes up—as they have a habit of so doing . . . Plenty of suitable merchant ships exist for conversion—if a "new build" was unacceptable. If such a ship were built or converted the RFA would be the obvious operators—and it could even be based on the Thames if no overseas commitment existed (a rare event). She could well be used as "home" to the huge team of naval personnel working in the Ministry of Defence and forced to find expensive lodgings in the city. With shore jobs almost unknown within the RFA there would be a long list of volunteers to man such a ship!

Whilst crystal ball gazing it is difficult to see how the RFA is to support the Royal Navy in its worldwide role in ten years time—now that a policy of "all your eggs in one basket" is to be persued. Doubtless the new "one stop" AOR's will be fine ships but with only two ordered and little sign of any more on, or over, the horizon the situation in a few years time could be critical. By then old faithful tankers such as the one remaining TIDE and the "OL" class will have been retired—or vast amounts of money invested in them to keep them operational. The Rover Class will be coming to the end of their working lives and only the large freighting tankers would remain. Unless the ships of the Royal Navy are to be employed as a coastal defence force it is difficult to see how commitments are to be met. Given the requirement to support the Falklands force, the West Indies Guardship, the Armilla Patrol in the Gulf, the Greenland/Iceland/UK Gap Patrol—before any exercises and overseas deployments are considered—it can easily be seen that commitments must be given up or new RFA ships ordered for the late 1990's. They don't come from builders overnight—but unexpected commitments frequently do come within that time scale.

The decline of the merchant navy is well known—the RFA managers have always had in the back of their minds that, should the requirement exist, they can always charter extra tanker tonnage on the commercial market. Unless the Royal Naval Fleet is to be supported by a Panamanian tanker with Greek officers and a Honduran crew now is the time to "stop the rot" within our own merchant service. The ability to charter suitable UK tonnage in a few years time will simply not be an option.

During a recent exercise old salts would have not believed the amount of merchant tonnage chartered to support a NATO exercise—with little sign of the red duster.

Whilst one would not wish to see one pound extra spent on "support services" rather than the front line units—it is a fact of life that without the ships of the RFA the naval fleet is unable to operate far from the home base. We disregard them—and their replacements—at our peril.

# SHIPS OF THE ROYAL FLEET AUXILIARY
## Pennant Numbers

| Ship | Penn No. | Ship | Penn No. | Ship | Penn No. |
|------|------|------|------|------|------|
| TIDESPRING | A75 | DILIGENCE | A132 | RESOURCE | A480 |
| APPLELEAF | A79 | ARGUS | A135 | REGENT | A486 |
| BRAMBLELEAF | A81 | GREEN ROVER | A268 | ENGADINE | K08 |
| BAYLEAF | A109 | GREY ROVER | A269 | SIR BEDIVERE | L3004 |
| ORANGELEAF | A110 | BLUE ROVER | A270 | SIR GALAHAD | L3005 |
| OAKLEAF | A111 | GOLD ROVER | A271 | SIR GERAINT | L3027 |
| OLWEN | A122 | BLACK ROVER | A273 | SIR LANCELOT | L3029 |
| OLNA | A123 | FORT GRANGE | A385 | SIR PERCIVALE | L3036 |
| OLMEDA | A124 | FORT AUSTIN | A386 | SIR TRISTRAM | L3505 |

● OFFICIAL PHOTO

**RFA Olwen**

## 'OL' CLASS

| Ship | Pennant Number | Completion Date | Builder |
|------|----------------|-----------------|---------|
| OLWEN | A122 | 1965 | Hawthorn Leslie |
| OLNA | A123 | 1966 | Hawthorn Leslie |
| OLMEDA | A124 | 1965 | Swan Hunter |

**Displacement** 36,000 tons **Dimensions** 197m x 26m x 10m **Speed** 19 knots **Complement** 92.

### Notes
These ships can operate up to 3 Sea King helicopters. Dry stores can be carried—and transferred at sea—as well as a wide range of fuel, aviation spirit and lubricants.

TANKERS

S. TALTON

**RFA Tidespring**

## TIDE CLASS

| Ship | Pennant Number | Completion Date | Builder |
|------|---------------|-----------------|---------|
| TIDESPRING | A75 | 1963 | Hawthorn Leslie |

**Displacement** 27,400 tons **Dimensions** 177m x 22m x 10m **Speed** 18 knots **Complement** 98.

**Notes**
Built to fuel warships at sea in any part of the world including strengthening for ice operations. A hangar and flight deck provides space for two Sea King helicopters if required. Was due to be "retired early" during 1982/3 but reprieved for Falklands crisis and remains in service but has only a limited career after 25 years service.

**RFA Green Rover**

## ROVER CLASS

| Ship | Pennant Number | Completion Date | Builder |
|------|----------------|-----------------|---------|
| GREEN ROVER ● | A268 | 1969 | Swan Hunter |
| GREY ROVER | A269 | 1970 | Swan Hunter |
| BLUE ROVER | A270 | 1970 | Swan Hunter |
| GOLD ROVER | A271 | 1974 | Swan Hunter |
| BLACK ROVER | A273 | 1974 | Swan Hunter |

**Displacement** 11,522 tons **Dimensions** 141m x 19m x 7m **Speed** 18 knots **Complement** 49-54.

### Notes
Small Fleet Tankers designed to supply HM ships with fresh water, dry cargo and refrigerated provisions as well as a range of fuel and lubricants. Helicopter deck but no hangar. ● In reserve.

**RFA Oakleaf**

## LEAF CLASS

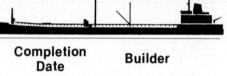

| Ship | Pennant Number | Completion Date | Builder |
|------|----------------|-----------------|---------|
| APPLELEAF | A79 | 1980 | Cammell Laird |
| BRAMBLELEAF | A81 | 1980 | Cammell Laird |
| BAYLEAF | A109 | 1982 | Cammell Laird |
| ORANGELEAF | A110 | 1982 | Cammell Laird |
| OAKLEAF | A111 | 1981 | Uddevalla |

**Displacement** 37,747 tons **Dimensions** 170m x 26m x 12m **Speed** 14.5 knots **Complement** 60.

**Notes**
All are ex merchant ships. BRAMBLELEAF is owned by MOD (N), the remainder are on bare boat charter. OAKLEAF (ex OKTANIA) differs from the other ships of the class which are all commercial Stat 32 tankers. At 49,310 tons she is the largest vessel in RFA/RN service.

66

**RFA Fort Grange**

## FORT CLASS

| Ship | Pennant Number | Completion Date | Builder |
|------|----------------|-----------------|---------|
| FORT GRANGE | A385 | 1978 | Scott Lithgow |
| FORT AUSTIN | A386 | 1979 | Scott Lithgow |

**Displacement** 23,384 tons **Dimensions** 183m x 24m x 9m **Speed** 20 knots **Complement** 201, (120 RFA, 36 RNSTS & 45 RN).

### Notes
Full hangar and maintenance facilities are provided and up to four Sea King helicopters can be carried for both the transfer of stores and anti-submarine protection of a group of ships. Both ships can be armed with 4 x 20mm guns mounted on the Scot platforms. Both are fitted with 3″ Chaff Systems.
The first of a new class of "one stop" ships to be named FORT VICTORIA is under construction at Belfast.

STORE SHIPS

● HMS OSPREY

# RFA Regent

## REGENT CLASS

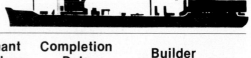

| Ship | Pennant Number | Completion Date | Builder |
|------|----------------|-----------------|---------|
| RESOURCE | A480 | 1967 | Scotts |
| REGENT | A486 | 1967 | Harland & Wolff |

**Displacement** 22,890 **Dimensions** 195m x 24m x 8m **Speed** 21 knots **Complement** 182, (RFA 112, RNSTS 37, RN 11).

### Notes
The widest range of naval armament stores are carried onboard plus a limited range of general naval stores and food. When the Wessex 5 was withdrawn from service in April 1987 both ships lost their permanently embarked helicopter but they retain full flight deck facilities.

68

**RFA Sir Percivale**

## LANDING SHIPS
## SIR LANCELOT CLASS

| Ship | Pennant Number | Completion Date | Builder |
|------|---------------|-----------------|---------|
| SIR BEDIVERE | L3004 | 1967 | Hawthorn |
| SIR GERAINT | L3027 | 1967 | Stephen |
| SIR LANCELOT | L3029 | 1964 | Fairfield |
| SIR PERCIVALE | L3036 | 1968 | Hawthorn |
| SIR TRISTRAM | L3505 | 1967 | Hawthorn |
| SIR GALAHAD | L3005 | 1987 | Swan Hunter |

**Displacement** 5,550 tons **Dimensions** 126m x 18m x 4m **Speed** 17 knots **Armament** Can be fitted with 2 x 40mm guns in emergency **Complement** 65, SIR GALAHAD (8,451 tons. 140m x 20m Complement 58.)

**Notes**
Manned by the RFA but tasked by the Army, these ships are used for heavy secure transport of stores—embarked by bow and stern doors —and beach assault landings. Can operate helicopters from tank deck if required. SIR LANCELOT is the last remaining RFA with a Hong Kong Chinese crew.

**RFA Diligence**

| Ship | Pennant Number | Completion Date | Builder |
|------|----------------|-----------------|---------|
| DILIGENCE | A132 | 1981 | Oresundsvarvet |

**Displacement** 5,814 tons **Dimensions** 120m x 12m **Speed** 15 knots **Armament** 2 x 20mm **Complement** RFA 40. RN Personnel — approx 100.

**Notes**
Formerly the M/V Stena Inspector purchased (£25m) for service in the South Atlantic. Accommodation is provided for a 100 man Fleet Maintenance Unit. Her deep diving complex was removed and workshops added. Deployed to Oman to support RN ships operating in the Gulf in late 1987 and remains on station.

**RFA Argus**

| Ship | Pennant Number | Completion Date | Builder |
|------|----------------|-----------------|---------|
| ARGUS | A135 | 1981 | Cantieri Navali Breda |

**Displacement** 28,081 tons (full load) **Dimensions** 175m x 30m x 8m **Speed** 18 knots **Armament** 4 x 30mm. 2 x 20mm **Complement** 254 (inc 137 Air Group) **Aircraft** 6 Sea King, 12 Harriers can be carried in a "ferry role".

**Notes**
Formerly the M/V CONTENDER BEZANT taken up from trade during the Falklands crisis. Purchased in 1984 (£13 million) for conversion to an 'Aviation Training Ship'. A £50 million re-build was undertaken at Belfast from 1984-87. Part IV trials have taken over a year but she will eventually (1989) replace ENGADINE when fully operational and operate from Portland.

SPECIAL SHIPS

● HMS OSPREY

**RFA Engadine**

| Ship | Pennant Number | Completion Date | Builder |
|------|----------------|-----------------|---------|
| ENGADINE | K08 | 1967 | Robb |

**Displacement** 9000 tons **Dimensions** 129m x 17m x 7m **Speed** 16 knots **Complement** 175 (73 RFA + up to 102 RN personnel).

**Notes**
Specially built for RFA service (but with embarked RN personnel) to provide training ship for helicopter crews operating in deep waters well away from coasts. Can operate up to 4 Sea Kings or 5 Lynx and often embarks pilotless target aircraft for exercises. Due to be deleted from the RFA list in mid 1988 but remains in service until ARGUS is operational.

# ROYAL MARITIME AUXILIARY SERVICE

The Royal Maritime Auxiliary Service Fleet is comprised of over 500 hulls, of which 310 are self propelled, including small harbour launches, the remainder being dumb craft such as lighters etc. It is administered by the Director of Marine Services (Naval) to whom the Captains of the Ports and Resident Naval Officers at the various Naval Bases are mainly responsible for the provision of Marine Services to the Royal Navy. The RMAS also provides many types of craft for the numerous and diverse requirements of other Ministry of Defence departments.

Ships of the RMAS, which can be seen at work in all the Naval Bases throughout the United Kingdom and at Gibraltar, are easily identified by their black hulls, buff coloured superstructure and funnels, and by the RMAS flag, which is a blue ensign defaced in the fly by a yellow anchor over two wavy lines. Pennant numbers are painted only on those vessels that are normally employed outside harbour limits.

● A. MASON                    **Dog Class Tugs in formation at Faslane**

The largest section of the fleet is employed on harbour duties, the types of vesels involved being Berthing and Tractor Tugs, Fleet Tenders, Tank Cleaning Lighters, Harbour Launches, Naval Armament Vessels and dumb lighters for carrying explosive stores, general stores, fuel, water and victuals to the Royal Navy, NATO Navies and Royal Fleet Auxiliary ships when they are in port or at anchor. In keeping with the Director of Marine Services policy of multi-role vessels, many of the larger units of the fleet have been modified to back up the harbour fleet when required.

A smaller section of the fleet is, however, engaged in a purely sea-going capacity. Ocean Tugs, Torpedo Recovery Vessels and Mooring and Salvage Vessels are designed and equipped for world wide towing and complex Marine Salvage operations. Experimental Trials Vessels, fitted with some of the most sophisticated modern equipment, are deployed on a wide range of duties in the fast growing area of advanced experimental technology necessary for the design of new warships, weapon systems and machinery.

Problems associated with the control and treatment of oil pollution at sea have become more pressing in recent years. To deal with emergencies in Dockyard Ports and to assist the Department of Transport with those that may arise around the coastline of the United Kingdom, the RMAS has adapted many of its vessels to carry chemical dispersants and the necessary spraying equipent. A review is underway however to ascertain if it would be more cost-effective for this task to be carried out by commercial contractors.

The size and composition of the RMAS Fleet is under constant review to ensure its compatibility with the changing requirements of the Royal Navy, which it exists to serve. Older units are being phased out, at times without replacement, and the introduction of new more versatile vessels will continue to provide savings in the total number of ships required.

With the size of the Royal Naval Fleet slowly getting smaller it is only right that the size of the RMAS should be reduced accordingly—but this is frequently difficult to achieve. A steady flow of reviews in recent years have been instigated and savings undoubtedly made—particularly in the field of manpower. Under the threat of commercialisation, limited reductions have been made and doubtless others could be made—once the navy's firm requirement for support services are known.

Undoubtedly RMAS vessels provide an excellent, albeit expensive, service to the Royal Navy but, in these days of an ever decreasing defence budget overheads must be reduced if the service is to keep its many vessels and loyal workforce. Further economies must be made and those vessels easily replaced by commercial tonnage in time of national crisis deleted from the RMAS fleet. The considerable savings are desperately needed elsewhere within the naval budget for "frontline" activities.

The RMAS have provided an excellent back up to the Royal Navy over the years—but, from all reports, they have paid "over the odds" for a service which, for understandable reasons, has frequently been under-employed in naval bases that now see fewer ships visiting or entering for refit.

# SHIPS OF THE ROYAL MARITIME AUXILIARY SERVICE — PENNANT NUMBERS

| Ship | Penn. No. | Ship | Penn. No. |
|---|---|---|---|
| MELTON | A83 | KATHLEEN | A166 |
| MENAI | A84 | EXPRESS | A167 |
| MEON | A87 | LABRADOR | A168 |
| MILFORD | A91 | KITTY | A170 |
| BEMBRIDGE | A101 | LESLEY | A172 |
| ALSATIAN | A106 | DOROTHY | A173 |
| FELICITY | A112 | LILAH | A174 |
| MAGNET | A114 | MARY | A175 |
| LODESTONE | A115 | EDITH | A177 |
| CAIRN | A126 | HUSKY | A178 |
| TORRENT | A127 | MASTIFF | A180 |
| TORRID | A128 | IRENE | A181 |
| DALMATION | A129 | SALUKI | A182 |
| TORNADO | A140 | ISABEL | A183 |
| TORCH | A141 | SALMOOR | A185 |
| TORMENTOR | A142 | SALMASTER | A186 |
| TOREADOR | A143 | SALMAID | A187 |
| DAISY | A145 | POINTER | A188 |
| WATERMAN | A146 | SETTER | A189 |
| FRANCES | A147 | JOAN | A190 |
| FIONA | A148 | JOYCE | A193 |
| FLORENCE | A149 | GWENDOLINE | A196 |
| GENEVIEVE | A150 | SEALYHAM | A197 |
| GEORGINA | A152 | HELEN | A198 |
| EXAMPLE | A153 | MYRTLE | A199 |
| EXPLORER | A154 | SPANIEL | A201 |
| DEERHOUND | A155 | NANCY | A202 |
| DAPHNE | A156 | NORAH | A205 |
| LOYAL HELPER | A157 | LLANDOVERY | A207 |
| SUPPORTER | A158 | LAMLASH | A208 |
| LOYAL WATCHER | A159 | CHARLOTTE | A210 |
| LOYAL VOLUNTEER | A160 | LECHLADE | A211 |
| LOYAL MEDIATOR | A161 | ENDEAVOUR | A213 |
| ELKHOUND | A162 | BEE | A216 |
| EXPLOIT | A163 | CHRISTINE | A217 |
| GOOSANDER | A164 | LOYAL | |
| POCHARD | A165 | MODERATOR | A220 |

| Ship | Penn. No. | Ship | Penn. No. |
|---|---|---|---|
| FORCEFUL | A221 | WARDEN | A368 |
| NIMBLE | A222 | KINTERBURY | A378 |
| POWERFUL | A223 | THROSK | A379 |
| ADEPT | A224 | CRICKLADE | A381 |
| BUSTLER | A225 | ST GEORGE | A382 |
| CAPABLE | A226 | CLOVELLY | A389 |
| CAREFUL | A227 | CRICCIETH | A391 |
| FAITHFUL | A228 | GLENCOE | A392 |
| CRICKET | A229 | DUNSTER | A393 |
| COCKCHAFER | A230 | FINTRY | A394 |
| DEXTEROUS | A231 | GRASMERE | A402 |
| GNAT | A239 | KINLOSS | A482 |
| SHEEPDOG | A250 | CROMARTY | A488 |
| LYDFORD | A251 | DORNOCH | A490 |
| DORIS | A252 | ROLLICKER | A502 |
| LADYBIRD | A253 | HEADCORN | A1766 |
| MEAVEY | A254 | HEVER | A1767 |
| CICALA | A263 | HARLECH | A1768 |
| SCARAB | A272 | HAMBLEDON | A1769 |
| KINBRACE | A281 | LOYAL | |
| AURICULA | A285 | CHANCELLOR | A1770 |
| ILCHESTER | A308 | LOYAL PROCTOR | A1771 |
| INSTOW | A309 | HOLMWOOD | A1772 |
| FOXHOUND | A326 | HORNING | A1773 |
| BASSET | A327 | MANDARIN | P192 |
| COLLIE | A328 | GARGANEY | P194 |
| CORGI | A330 | GOLDENEYE | P195 |
| FOTHERBY | A341 | ALNMOUTH | Y13 |
| FELSTEAD | A348 | WATERFALL | Y17 |
| CARTMEL | A350 | WATERSHED | Y18 |
| ELKSTONE | A353 | WATERSPOUT | Y19 |
| FROXFIELD | A354 | WATERSIDE | Y20 |
| EPWORTH | A355 | OILPRESS | Y21 |
| ROYSTERER | A361 | OILSTONE | Y22 |
| DOLWEN | A362 | OILWELL | Y23 |
| DENMEAD | A363 | OILFIELD | Y24 |
| WHITEHEAD | A364 | OILBIRD | Y25 |
| FULBECK | A365 | OILMAN | Y26 |
| ROBUST | A366 | WATERCOURSE | Y30 |
| NEWTON | A367 | WATERFOWL | Y31 |

OFFICIAL PHOTO **RMAS Robust**

## ROYSTERER CLASS

| Ship | Pennant Number | Completion Date | Builder |
| --- | --- | --- | --- |
| ROYSTERER | A361 | 1972 | C.D. Holmes |
| ROBUST | A366 | 1974 | C.D. Holmes |
| ROLLICKER | A502 | 1973 | C.D. Holmes |

**G.R.T.** 1,036 tons **Dimensions** 54m x 12m x 6m **Speed** 15 knots **Complement** 21.

**Notes**
Built for salvage and long range towage, but are frequently used for various "deepwater" trials. The tug TYPHOON was deleted from the RMAS fleet in late 1988.

T
U
G
S

W. SARTORI

RMAS Powerful

## HARBOUR TUGS
## TWIN UNIT TRACTOR TUGS (TUTT'S)

| Ship | Pennant Number | Completion Date | Builder |
| --- | --- | --- | --- |
| FORCEFUL | A221 | 1985 | R. Dunston |
| NIMBLE | A222 | 1985 | R. Dunston |
| POWERFUL | A223 | 1985 | R. Dunston |
| ADEPT | A224 | 1980 | R. Dunston |
| BUSTLER | A225 | 1981 | R. Dunston |
| CAPABLE | A226 | 1981 | R. Dunston |
| CAREFUL | A227 | 1982 | R. Dunston |
| FAITHFUL | A228 | 1985 | R. Dunston |
| DEXTEROUS | A231 | 1986 | R. Dunston |

**G.R.T.** 375 tons **Dimensions** 39m x 10m x 4m **Speed** 12 knots **Complement** 9

**Notes**
The principle harbour tug in naval service. CAPABLE is at Gibraltar.

**RMAS Alsatian**

## DOG CLASS

| Ship | Penn. No. | Ship | Penn. No. |
|---|---|---|---|
| ALSATIAN | A106 | POINTER | A188 |
| CAIRN ● | A126 | SETTER | A189 |
| DALMATIAN | A129 | SEALYHAM | A197 |
| DEERHOUND | A155 | SPANIEL | A201 |
| ELKHOUND | A162 | SHEEPDOG | A250 |
| LABRADOR | A168 | FOXHOUND | A326 |
| HUSKY | A178 | BASSET | A327 |
| MASTIFF | A180 | COLLIE ● | A328 |
| SALUKI | A182 | CORGI | A330 |

**G.R.T.** 152 tons **Dimensions** 29m x 8m x 4m **Speed** 12 knots **Complement** 5

**Notes**
General harbour tugs — all completed between 1962 & 1972.
● No longer tugs. Refitted as trials vessels for service at Kyle of Lochalsh.
The long term replacement of these vessels is now under discussion within the Ministry.

W. SARTORI

**RMAS Dorothy**

## IMPROVED GIRL CLASS

| Ship | Penn. No. | Ship | Penn. No. |
|------|-----------|------|-----------|
| DAISY | A145 | CHARLOTTE | A210 |
| DAPHNE | A156 | CHRISTINE | A217 |
| DOROTHY | A173 | DORIS | A252 |
| EDITH | A177 | | |

**G.R.T.** 75 tons **Speed** 10 knots **Complement** 4

**Notes**
All completed 1971-2.

W. SARTORI

**RMAS Norah**

## IRENE CLASS

| Ship | Penn. No. | Ship | Penn. No. |
|---|---|---|---|
| KATHLEEN | A166 | ISABEL | A183 |
| KITTY | A170 | JOAN | A190 |
| LESLEY | A172 | JOYCE | A193 |
| LILAH | A174 | MYRTLE | A199 |
| MARY | A175 | NANCY | A202 |
| IRENE | A181 | NORAH | A205 |

**G.R.T.** 89 tons **Speed** 8 knots **Complement** 4

**Notes**
Known as Water Tractors these craft are used for basin moves and towage of light barges.

81

**RMAS Helen**

## FELICITY CLASS

| Ship | Penn. No. | Ship | Penn. No. |
|------|-----------|------|-----------|
| FELICITY | A112 | GENEVIEVE | A150 |
| FRANCES | A147 | GEORGINA | A152 |
| FIONA | A148 | GWENDOLINE | A196 |
| FLORENCE | A149 | HELEN | A198 |

**G.R.T.** 80 tons **Speed** 10 knots **Complement** 4

**Notes**
Water Tractors — completed in 1973; FRANCES, FLORENCE & GENEVIEVE completed 1980.

82

M. LENNON

**RMAS Whitehead**

## TRIALS SHIPS

| Ship | Pennant Number | Completion Date | Builder |
|------|----------------|-----------------|---------|
| WHITEHEAD | A364 | 1971 | Scotts |

**G.R.T.** 3,427 tons **Dimensions** 97m x 15m x 5m **Speed** 15.5 knots **Complement** 38

**Notes**
Fitted with Torpedo Tubes for trial firings. A planned "mid-life" refit was postponed in 1988. Her future is now expected to be decided in early 1989.

T
R
I
A
L
S

S
H
I
P
S

M. LENNON

**RMAS Newton**

| Ship | Pennant Number | Completion Date | Builder |
|------|----------------|-----------------|---------|
| NEWTON | A367 | 1976 | Scotts |

**G.R.T.** 2,779 tons **Dimensions** 99m x 16m x 6m **Speed** 15 knots **Complement** 39

**Notes**
Built as sonar propagation trials ship but can also be used as a Cable Layer.

**RMAS Auricula**

## TEST & EXPERIMENTAL SONAR TENDER

| Ship | Pennant Number | Completion Date | Builder |
|------|----------------|-----------------|---------|
| AURICULA | A285 | 1981 | Ferguson Bros |

**G.R.T.** 981 tons **Dimensions** 52m x 11m x 3m **Speed** 12 knots **Complement** 20

### Notes
Employed on evaluation work of new sonar equipment that may equip RN ships of the future. Based at Portland.

OFFICIAL PHOTO **RMAS St George**

## ARMAMENT STORES CARRIERS

| Ship | Pennant Number | Completion Date | Builder |
|------|----------------|-----------------|---------|
| KINTERBURY | A378 | 1980 | Appledore SB |
| THROSK | A379 | 1977 | Cleland SB Co. |
| ST GEORGE | A382 | 1981 | Appledore SB |

**G.R.T.** 1,357 tons **Dimensions** 64m x 12m x 5m **Speed** 14 knots **Complement** 19

**Notes**
2 holds carry Naval armament stores, ammunition and guided missiles. All three vessels vary slightly. ST GEORGE taken over in late 1988 from the Army and will be re-named in 1989. Only KINTERBURY operational, others in reserve at Portsmouth.

M. LENNON

RMAS Scarab

## INSECT CLASS

| Ship | Pennant Number | Completion Date | Builder |
| --- | --- | --- | --- |
| BEE | A216 | 1970 | C.D. Holmes |
| CRICKET | A229 | 1972 | Beverley |
| COCKCHAFER | A230 | 1971 | Beverley |
| GNAT | A239 | 1972 | Beverley |
| LADYBIRD | A253 | 1973 | Beverley |
| CICALA | A263 | 1971 | Beverley |
| SCARAB | A272 | 1973 | Beverley |

**G.R.T.** 279 tons **Dimensions** 34m x 8m x 3m **Speed** 10.5 knots **Complement** 7-9

**Notes**
CRICKET and SCARAB are fitted as Mooring Vessels and COCKCHAFER as a Trials Stores Carrier — remainder are Naval Armament carriers.

TENDERS

**RNXS Loyal Mediator**

## LOYAL CLASS

| Ship | Penn. No. | Ship | Penn. No. |
|---|---|---|---|
| LOYAL HELPER | A157 | LOYAL MEDIATOR | A161 |
| SUPPORTER | A158 | LOYAL MODERATOR | A220 |
| LOYAL WATCHER | A159 | LOYAL CHANCELLOR | A1770 |
| LOYAL VOLUNTEER | A160 | LOYAL PROCTOR | A1771 |

**G.R.T.** 112 tons **Dimensions** 24m x 6m x 3m **Speed** 10.5 knots **Complement** 24

### Notes
All these craft are operated by the Royal Naval Auxiliary Service (RNXS)—men (and women)—who in time of emergency would man these craft for duties as port control vessels.

**RMAS Llandovery**

## (TYPE A, B & X) TENDERS

| Ship | Penn. No. | Ship | Penn. No. |
|---|---|---|---|
| MELTON | A83 | FULBECK | A365 |
| MENAI | A84 | CRICKLADE | A381 |
| MEON | A87 | CLOVELLY | A389 |
| MILFORD | A91 | CRICCIETH | A391 |
| LLANDOVERY | A207 | GLENCOE | A392 |
| LAMLASH | A208 | DUNSTER | A393 |
| LECHLADE | A211 | FINTRY | A394 |
| LYDFORD | A251 | GRASMERE | A402 |
| MEAVEY | A254 | CROMARTY | A488 |
| ILCHESTER* | A308 | DORNOCH | A490 |
| INSTOW* | A309 | HEADCORN | A1766 |
| FOTHERBY | A341 | HEVER | A1767 |
| FELSTEAD | A348 | HARLECH | A1768 |
| ELKSTONE | A353 | HAMBLEDON | A1769 |
| FROXFIELD | A354 | HOLMWOOD | A1772 |
| EPWORTH | A355 | HORNING | A1773 |
| DENMEAD | A363 | DATCHET | A357 |

**G.R.T.** 78 tons **Dimensions** 24m x 6m x 3m **Speed** 10.5 knots **Complement** 4/5

### Notes

All completed since 1971 to replace Motor Fishing Vessels. Vessels marked* are diving tenders. Remainder are Training Tenders, Passenger Ferries, or Cargo Vessels. GLENCOE is on loan to the RNXS—based at Portsmouth—and painted grey.

M. LENNON

**RMAS Alnmouth**

## ABERDOVEY CLASS ('63 DESIGN)

| Ship | Penn. No. | Ship | Penn. No. |
|------|-----------|------|-----------|
| ALNMOUTH | Y13 | CARTMEL | A350 |
| BEMBRIDGE | A101 | | |

**G.R.T.** 77 tons **Dimensions** 24m x 5m x 3m **Speed** 10.5 knots **Complement** 4/5

### Notes
ALNMOUTH is a Sea Cadet Training Ship based at Plymouth, BEMBRIDGE at Portsmouth. CARTMEL is on loan to the RNXS based on the Clyde. Other vessels of the class now used by Sea Cadet/RNR Units.

**XSV Explorer**

## COASTAL TRAINING CRAFT
## EXAMPLE CLASS

| Ship | Pennant Number | Completion Date | Builder |
|------|----------------|-----------------|---------|
| XSV EXAMPLE | A153 | 1985 | Watercraft |
| XSV EXPLORER | A154 | 1985 | Watercraft |
| XSV EXPLOIT | A163 | 1988 | Vosper T |
| XSV EXPRESS | A167 | 1988 | Vosper T |

**Displacement** 43 tons **Dimensions** 20m x 6m x 1m **Speed** 20 knots
**Armament** Nil **Complement** 14

### Notes
Have replaced the former Inshore Minesweepers in RNXS
service. PORTISHAM retained for training role but 1989 is
expected to be her last year in service.

91

**RMAS Oilbird**

## OILPRESS CLASS

| Ship | Pennant Number | Completion Date | Builder |
| --- | --- | --- | --- |
| OILPRESS | Y21 | 1969 | Appledore Shipbuilders |
| OILSTONE | Y22 | 1969 | " " |
| OILWELL | Y23 | 1969 | " " |
| OILFIELD | Y24 | 1969 | " " |
| OILBIRD | Y25 | 1969 | " " |
| OILMAN | Y26 | 1969 | " " |

**G.R.T.** 362 tons **Dimensions** 41m x 9m x 3m **Speed** 11 knots **Complement** 5

### Notes
Employed as Harbour and Coastal Oilers. OILFIELD is in reserve at Portsmouth.

W. SARTORI                          **RMAS Waterman**

## WATER CARRIERS
## WATER CLASS

| Ship | Pennant Number | Completion Date | Builder |
|------|----------------|-----------------|---------|
| WATERFALL ● | Y17 | 1967 | Drypool Eng Co |
| WATERSHED | Y18 | 1967 | Drypool Eng Co |
| WATERSPOUT | Y19 | 1967 | Drypool Eng Co |
| WATERSIDE | Y20 | 1968 | Drypool Eng Co |
| WATERCOURSE | Y30 | 1974 | Drypool Eng Co |
| WATERFOWL | Y31 | 1974 | Drypool Eng Co |
| WATERMAN | A146 | 1978 | R. Dunston |

**G.R.T.** 263 tons **Dimensions** 40m x 8m x 2m **Speed** 11 knots
**Complement** 5

### Notes
Capable of coastal passages, these craft normally supply either
demineralised or fresh water to the Fleet within port limits.
● laid up at Portsmouth being beyond economic repair.

93

M. LENNON

**RMAS Magnet**

## DEGAUSSING VESSELS
## MAGNET CLASS

| Ship | Pennant Number | Completion Date | Builder |
|------|----------------|-----------------|---------|
| MAGNET | A114 | 1979 | Cleland |
| LODESTONE | A115 | 1980 | Cleland |

**G.R.T.** 828 tons **Dimensions** 55m x 12m x 4m **Speed** 14 knots
**Complement** 9
**Notes**
One ship is normally operational, the other kept in reserve.

94

M. LENNON

**RMAS Torrid**

## TORPEDO RECOVERY VESSELS (TRV'S)
## TORRID CLASS

| Ship | Pennant Number | Completion Date | Builder |
|------|----------------|-----------------|---------|
| TORRENT | A127 | 1971 | Cleland SB Co |
| TORRID | A128 | 1972 | Cleland SB Co |

**G.R.T.** 550 tons **Dimensions** 46m x 9m x 3m **Speed** 12 knots
**Complement** 14

### Notes
A stern ramp is built for the recovery of torpedoes fired for trials
and exercises. A total of 32 can be carried.

**RMAS Tornado**

## TORNADO CLASS

| Ship | Pennant Number | Completion Date | Builder |
| --- | --- | --- | --- |
| TORNADO | A140 | 1979 | Hall Russell |
| TORCH | A141 | 1980 | Hall Russell |
| TORMENTOR | A142 | 1980 | Hall Russell |
| TOREADOR | A143 | 1980 | Hall Russell |

**G.R.T.** 560 tons **Dimensions** 47m x 8m x 3m **Speed** 14 knots **Complement** 13

**Notes**
TORCH is based at Portland, TORMENTOR at Plymouth — remainder on the Clyde.

W. SARTORI

**RMAS Salmoor**

## SAL CLASS

| Ship | Pennant Number | Completion Date | Builder |
|---|---|---|---|
| SALMOOR | A185 | 1985 | Hall Russell |
| SALMASTER | A186 | 1986 | Hall Russell |
| SALMAID | A187 | 1986 | Hall Russell |

**Displacement** 2200 tonnes **Dimensions** 77m x 15m x 4m **Speed** 15 knots **Complement** 17

**Notes**
Built at a cost of £9 million each these ships have replaced the 40-year-old Kin class. They are multi-purpose vessels designed to lay and maintain underwater targets and moorings and undertake a wide range of salvage tasks.

M
S
V
's

W. SARTORI

## WILD DUCK CLASS

| Ship | Pennant Number | Completion Date | Builder |
|------|---------|----------|---------|
| MANDARIN | P192 | 1964 | C. Laird |
| GARGANEY | P194 | 1966 | Brooke Marine |
| GOLDENEYE | P195 | 1966 | Brooke Marine |
| GOOSANDER | A164 | 1973 | Robb Caledon |
| POCHARD | A165 | 1973 | Robb Caledon |

**G.R.T.** 900 tons* **Dimensions** 58mm x 12m x 4m **Speed** 10 knots
**Complement** 18
* Vessels vary slightly

**Notes**
Vessels capable of carrying out a wide range of duties laying moorings and heavy lift salvage work. 200 tons can be lifted over over the bow. MANDARIN brought forward from reserve in late 1988 to replace PINTAIL at Portland. The latter to be expended as a target.

**RMAS Kinloss**

## KIN CLASS

| Ship | Pennant Number | Completion Date | Builder |
| --- | --- | --- | --- |
| KINBRACE | A281 | 1944 | A. Hall Aberdeen |
| KINLOSS | A482 | 1945 | A. Hall Aberdeen |

**Displacement** 1,050 tons **Dimensions** 54m x 11m x 4m **Speed** 9 knots **Complement** 18

**Notes**

Coastal Salvage Vessels re-engined between 1963 & 1967. KINBRACE is now in reserve at Portsmouth and KINLOSS has a trials role at Rosyth but the two vessels will exchange roles during 1989. Two 32 metre Powered Mooring Lighters are being built (by McTay Marine) for completion during 1989. They will be named MOORFOWL and MOORHEN.

M. LENNON

**RMAS Dolwen**

## DOLWEN CLASS

| Ship | Pennant Number | Completion Date | Builder |
|---|---|---|---|
| DOLWEN (ex Hector Gulf) | A362 | 1962 | P.K. Harris |

**Displacement** 602 tons **Dimensions** 41m x 9m x 4m **Speed** 14 knots **Complement** 11

**Notes**
Built as a stern trawler, then purchased for use as a Buoy tender — now used as a Range Mooring Vessel for RAE ABERPORTH (S. Wales) from her base at Pembroke Dock. Will be replaced in the RMAS Fleet in 1989 once WARDEN is operational.

100

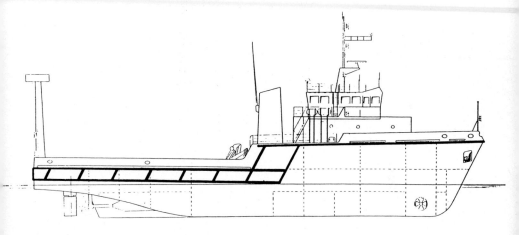

**RMAS Warden**

## WARDEN CLASS

| Ship | Pennant Number | Completion Date | Builder |
|------|----------------|-----------------|---------|
| WARDEN | A368 | 1989 | Richards |

**Displacement** 626 tons **Dimensions** 48m x 10m x4m **Speed** 15 knots **Complement**

**Notes**
Due for completion in mid 1989 to replace DOLWEN.

● MOD (ARMY)

**HMAV Ardennes**

## ARMY LANDING CRAFT

**LCL CLASS**                    **LANDING CRAFT LOGISTIC**

| Vessel | Pennant Number | Completion Date | Builder |
|---|---|---|---|
| HMAV Ardennes | L4001 | 1977 | Brooke Marine |
| HMAV Arakan | L4003 | 1978 | Brooke Marine |

**Displacement** 1,050 tons **Dimensions** 72m x 15m x 2m **Speed** 10 knots **Complement** 36

### Notes
Designed to carry up to 520 tonnes of cargo, overside loaded, or up to Five Chieftain tanks—Ro Ro laoded, reducing to 254 tonnes for beaching opreations, through bow doors. Priicapal roles are maintenance of the Royal Artillery Range Outer Hebrides and in support of Amphibious Operations and Exercises.

M. LOUAGIE

**RCTV Andalsnes**

## RCL CLASS

## RAMPED CRAFT LOGISTIC

| Vessel | Pennant Number | Completion Date | Builder |
|---|---|---|---|
| RCTV Arromanches | L105 | 1981 | Brooke Marine |
| RCTV Antwerp | L106 | 1981 | Brooke Marine |
| RCTV Andalsnes | L107 | 1984 | James & Stone |
| RCTV Abbeville | L108 | 1985 | James & Stone |
| RCTV Akyab | L109 | 1985 | James & Stone |
| RCTV Aachen | L110 | 1986 | McTay Marine |
| RCTV Arezzo | L111 | 1986 | McTay Marine |
| RCTV Agheila | L112 | 1987 | McTay Marine |
| RCTV Audemer | L113 | 1987 | McTay Marine |

**Displacement** 165 tons **Dimensions** 30m x 8m x 2m **Speed** 9 knots
**Complement** 6

**Notes**
Smaller—"all purpose" landing craft capable of carrying up to
100 tons. In service in coastal waters around Cyprus, Hong Kong
& UK.

# AIRCRAFT OF THE FLEET AIR ARM

## British Aerospace Sea Harrier

**Variants**: FRS 1 (FRS 2 undergoing development).
**Role**: Short take off, vertical landing (STOVL) fighter, reconnaissence and strike aircraft.
**Engine**: 1 x 21,500lb thrust Rolls Royce PEGASUS 104 turbojet.
**Span** 25'3" **length** 47'7" **height** 12'0" **max weight** 26,200lb.
**Max speed** Mach 1.2 **Crew** 1 pilot.
**Avionics**: Blue Fox pulse radar. (To be replaced by the Blue Vixen pulse doppler radar in the FRS 2).
**Armament**: SEA EAGLE air to surface missiles. SIDEWINDER air to air missiles. (FRS 2 to carry the new Anglo/US AMRAAM radar guided air to air missiles). 2 x 30mm Aden cannons with 120 rounds per gun in detachable pods, one either side of the lower fuselage. 1 fuselage centreline and 4 underwing hardpoints. The inner wing stations are capable of carrying 2,000lb of stores and are plumbed for drop tanks. The other positions can carry stores up to 1,000lb in weight. Possible loads include 1,000lb, 500lb or practice bombs; BL 755 cluster bombs, Lepus flares, 190 or 100 gallon drop tanks. A single F95 camera is mounted obliquely in the nose for the reconnaissence role. The prototype FRS 2 first flew in September 1988.
**Squadron Service**: 800, 801 and 899 squadrons in commission.
**Notes**: During 1989, 800 squadron will be embarked in HMS ILLUSTRIOUS and 801 in HMS ARK ROYAL. 899 squadron is responsible for the training of replacement pilots and the development of tactics and is normally shore based at RNAS YEOVILTON. In a period of tension it could embark to reinforce the embarked air groups in the carriers. Once HMS INVINCIBLE has completed post refit trials, 800 squadron will transfer to her from ILLUSTRIOUS.

# Westland SEA KING

Developed for the Royal Navy from the Sikorsky SH3D, the basic Seaking airframe is used in three different roles. The following details are common to all:
**Engines** 2 x 1600shp Rolls Royce Gnome H 1400—1 free power turbines.
**Rotor Diameter** 62′ 0″ **Length** 54′9″ **Height** 17′2″ **Max Weight** 23,500lb **Max Speed** 120 knots.

The 3 versions are:-

## HAS 5

**Roles**: Anti-submarine search and strike. SAR. Transport.
**Crew**: 2 pilots, 1 observer and 1 aircrewman.
**Avionics**: MEL Sea Searcher radar; Plessey Type 195 variable depth active/passive sonar. GEC LAPADS passive sonobuoy analyses. Marconi Orange Crop passive ESM equipment.
**Armament**: 4 fuselage hardpoints capable of carrying STINGRAY, Mk 46/Mk 44 torpedoes or depth charges. Various flares, markers, grenades and sonobuoys can be carried internally and hand launched. A 7.62mm machine gun can be mounted in the doorway.
**Squadron Service**: 706, 810, 814, 819, 820, 824 and 826 squadrons in commission.
**Notes**: The Seaking has been the backbone of the Fleet Air Arm's anti-submarine force since 1970. A further improved version, the HAS 6 is undergoing development. 706 is the advanced training squadron at RNAS CULDROSE. 810 is an operational training squadron with the capability to embark to reinforce the front line. During 1989, 814 squadron will be embarked in HMS ILLUSTRIOUS and 820 in HMS ARK ROYAL. 819 is shore based at PRESTWICK. 824 is a trials unit also based at HMS GANNET and 826 provides flights for service in RFA ships. The HAS 5 has a noteable SAR capability which is frequently demonstrated in the south west approaches. 814 squadron will transfer to HMS INVINCIBLE once she has completed post refit trials.

### AEW 2
**Role**: Airborne Early Warning. **Crew**: 1 pilot and 2 observers.
**Avionics**: Thorn/EMI searchwater radar. Marconi Orange Crop passive ESM equipment.
**Armament**: Nil.
**Squadron Service**: 849 HQ, 849A and 849B flights in commission.
**Notes**: Used to detect low flying aircraft trying to attack aircraft carrier battle groups under shipborne radar cover. Can also be used for surface search utilising its sophisticated, computerised long range radar. During 1989 849A flight will be embarked in HMS ILLUSTRIOUS and 849B in HMS ARK ROYAL. 849HQ acts as a training and trials unit at RNAS CULDROSE. 849A flight will transfer to HMS INVINCIBLE once she has completed post refit trials.

---

### HC 4
**Role**: Commando assault and utility transport.
**Avionics**: —
**Crew**: 1 pilot and 1 aircrewman.
**Armament**: Door mounted 7.62mm machine gun.
**Squadron Service**: 707, 845 and 846 squadrons in commission.
**Notes**: Capable of carrying up to 27 troops in the cabin or a wide variety of underslung loads up to 8,000lb in weight. 707 squadron is a training unit at RNAS YEOVILTON. 845 and 846 squadrons are based at YEOVILTON but able to embark or detach at short notice to support 3 Commando Brigade. The Sea King HC4 has a fixed undercarriage with no sponsons and no radome.

# Westland LYNX

**Variants**: HAS 2, HAS 3
**Roles**: Surface search and strike; anti-submarine strike; SAR.
**Engines**: 2 x 900hp Rolls Royce GEM BS 360-07-26 free shaft turbines.
**Rotor diameter**: 42'0" **Length** 39'1¼" **Height** 11' 0" **Max Weight** 9,500lb.
**Max Speed**: 150 knots. **Crew**: 1 pilot and 1 observer.
**Avionics**: Ferranti SEA SPRAY radar. Marconi Orange Crop passive ESM equipment.
**Armament**: External pylons carry up to 4 x SEA SKUA air to surface missiles or 2 x STINGRAY, Mk 46 or Mk 44 torpedoes, depth charges, flares or markers.
**Squadron Service**: 702, 815 and 829 squadrons in commission.
**Notes**: 702 is a training squadron based at RNAS PORTLAND. 815, also based at Portland is the parent unit for single aircraft flights that embark in Type 42 destroyers and some classes of frigate, specialising in the surface strike role. 829 squadron parents flights in the Type 22 and other anti-submarine frigates. A version of the Lynx, the AH1, is operated by the Royal Marines Brigade Air Squadron which is based at RNAS Yeovilton and an improved naval version of the Lynx is undergoing development.

## Westland GAZELLE HT2

**Engine**: 1 x 592shp Turbomeca ASTAZOU free power turbine.
**Crew**: 1 or 2 pilots.
**Notes**: In service with 705 squadron at RNAS CULDROSE. Used for training all RN helicopter pilots up to "wings standard" before they move onto the SeaKing or Lynx. A version of the Gazelle, the AH1, is used by the Royal Marines Brigade Air Squadron based at RNAS Yeovilton.

**de Havilland
Sea Devon**

# OTHER AIRCRAFT TYPES IN ROYAL NAVY SERVICE DURING 1989/90

### British Aerospace JETSTREAM T2 and T3
**Engines**: 2 x 940hp Turbomeca ASTAZOU 16D turboprops. (T3 Garrett turboprops).
**Crew**: 1 or 2 pilots, 2 student observers plus 3 other seats.
**Notes**: A number of these aircraft are used by 750 squadron at RNAS CULDROSE for training Fleet Air Arm Observers.

### de Havilland CHIPMUNK
**Engine**: 1 x 145hp de Havilland Gipsy Major 8 piston engine.
**Crew**: 2 pilots.
**Notes**: Used by the RN Flying Grading Flight at Roborough airport near Plymouth (and as such the first aircraft flown by generations of naval aircrew) and by stations flights at RNAS CULDROSE and YEOVILTON.

### de Havilland SEA DEVON
**Engines**: 2 x 340hp de Havilland Gipsy Queen 70 piston engines.
**Crew**: 1 pilot, 1 aircrewman and up to 8 passengers.
**Notes**: 2 of these veteran transport aircraft remain as part of 771 squadron at RNAS CULDROSE.

### de Havilland SEA HERON
**Engines**: 4 x 250hp de Havilland Gipsy Queen 30 piston engines.
**Crew**: 1 pilot, 1 aircrewman and up to 12 passengers.
**Notes**: In service since 1961, 4 of these excellent work horses remain in the station flight at RNAS YEOVILTON. They provide an inter-air station clipper service and support front line units with stores and transport.

## British Aerospace CANBERRA TT18

**Engines**: 2 x 6500lb thrust Rolls Royce AVON turbojets.
**Crew**: 1 pilot and 1 observer.
**Notes**: Used by the (civilian manned) Fleet Requirements and Aircraft Direction Unit (FRADU) at RNAS YEOVILTON. Canberras provide towed targets for live firings by ships at sea.

## Hawker HUNTER T8 and GA11

**Engine**: 1 x 7575lb thrust Rolls Royce AVON turbojet.
**Crew**: T8 1 or 2 pilots. GA11 1 pilot.
**Notes**: The Royal Navy has used Hunters to train fixed wing pilots since 1958. A number remain in service at RNAS YEOVILTON with the RN flying standards flight and with FRADU who use them as airborne targets for the aircraft direction school.

**In addition to these aircraft, the following aircraft have naval functions:**

**CANBERRA T17**: Used by 360 joint RN/RAF squadron for electronic warfare tasks. Based at RAF WYTON.

**British Aerospace 125**: Two aircraft, owned by the RN are operated by RN aircrew as part of 32 squadron RAF based at RAF NORTHOLT.

The Fleet Air Arm Historic flight based at RNAS YEOVILTON has a **SWORDFISH, SEAHAWK, SEAFURY, FIREFLY and TIGER MOTH** on strength and these are often seen at air displays in the summer months.

---

Full details of these and many other naval aircraft can be found in the new and completely revised edition of AIRCRAFT OF THE ROYAL NAVY SINCE 1945 published by Maritime Books..

# At the end of the line . . .

Readers may well find other warships afloat which are not mentioned in this book. The majority have fulfilled a long and useful life and are now relegated to non-seagoing duties. The following list gives details of their current duties:

| Penn. No. | Ship | Remarks |
| --- | --- | --- |
| C35 | BELFAST | World War II Cruiser Museum ship—Pool of London (Open to the public) |
| D73 | CAVALIER | World War II Destroyer. Museum Ship at Hebburn. Awaiting restoration. |
| D12 | KENT | County Class Destroyer—Sea Cadet Training Ship at Portsmouth Future "under consideration" |
| F39 | NAIAD | Static Trials Vessel—Portsmouth |
| F126 | PLYMOUTH | Type 12 Frigate Museum Ship at Plymouth. (Open to the public) |
| S11 | ORPHEUS | Oberon Class Submarine Harbour Training Ship at Gosport |
| S67 | ALLIANCE | Submarine Museum Ship at Gosport (Open to the public) |

**At the time of publishing the following ships were awaiting tow for scrap or sale.**

**PORTSMOUTH**
Berry Head
Rame Head
Leander
Londonderry
Falmouth
Stubbington
Maxton
Bronington

**MILFORD HAVEN**
Eskimo
Woodlark
(Targets)

**ROSYTH**
Dreadnought
Lofoten
Stalker

**PLYMOUTH**
Aurora

*A number of merchant ships are on charter to various MOD departments. They include MAERSK ASCENSION, MAERSK GANNET, ST BRANDAN, OIL MARINER & STENA SEASPREAD in support of the Falkland Island commitment. NORTHELLA, STARELLA and NORTHERN HORIZON have training/trials roles in UK waters.*

---

## NOTES

---

## PHOTOGRAPHERS

The selection of photographs for use in the next edition will be made in September. We only use pictures of ships underway—preferably without a background. Please send SAE if you want photographs returned.